IMAGES
of America

OCEANSIDE

I dedicate this book to Betty Dunwoody, an Oceanside treasure. Betty worked as a secretary in the Oceanside School District for 48 years and passed away in April 2004 after a long illness. During the last 25 years, as secretary for the high school's student projects, she helped to coordinate events such as Sports Night and Homecoming and clubs like DECA and Model Congress. Incredibly active, Betty was a golfer, a member of the Republican Club, and the first president of the Kiwanettes. She was tenacious and had a way of accomplishing tasks like no one else. She never took "No" for an answer when she asked someone for help, and she never said "No" when she was asked to help. When Betty saw me, her standard expression was, "Here comes trouble!" Then came laughs and conversation—and if I ever needed something, I would have it before I left. Loved by all, she is missed by all. (Courtesy of Pam DeBaun.)

IMAGES
of America

OCEANSIDE

Richard Woods

ARCADIA
PUBLISHING

Published by Arcadia Publishing
Charleston, South Carolina

Library of Congress Catalog Card Number: 2004108748

For all general information contact Arcadia Publishing at:
Telephone 843-853-2070
Fax 843-853-0044
E-mail sales@arcadiapublishing.com
For customer service and orders:
Toll-Free 1-888-313-2665

Visit us on the Internet at www.arcadiapublishing.com

Welcome to Oceanside. Oceanside is a middle-class suburb of New York City with approximately 33,000 residents. Here, the DeLucia sisters, c. 1940, beckon you to come inside and take a look at their town. From left to right, they are Mildred, Angela, and Mary. (Courtesy of Mike Franzini.)

CONTENTS

Oceansiders are proud of their town and not afraid to show it. Pictured here is a participating high school teacher at a ceremony celebrating a foreign-exchange program. Students from overseas came and stayed in Oceanside in order to learn about other cultures firsthand. (Courtesy of the Oceanside School District Archives.)

INTRODUCTION

I decided to write *Oceanside* after attending the first Circle of Pride inductions in the spring of 2003. At the ceremony, Oceanside's finest athletes and coaches were installed as members of a special section of the high school's Athletic Hall of Fame. The event drew 300 people and turned away more. The goodwill and warm feeling in the room that night inspired me. I wanted to write this book to give the town where I grew up the recognition it deserves.

The best part of putting the book together was meeting so many great people. It made me realize that, in many ways, Oceanside still is a small town, a community that cares. Significant and colorful, its history began before most other Nassau County communities existed. As I researched the past, I found that certain themes developed. Oceanside is made up of families who care about their children and their neighborhood. Throughout its history, the glue holding the community together has been its religious institutions, its fire department, its school district, and its great families.

This book is not the first to be written about Oceanside. Frances Heinley Weaver, an English teacher at the high school, wrote an excellent history up to 1940. Later, Walter Boardman credited Weaver when he republished much of her work in *The Story of Oceanside*. In the 1970s the First Methodist Church and the Jewish youth group Aleph Zadik Aleph published a book containing Weaver's work plus some updated information. More recently, the historical group The Oceanside Foundation republished Boardman's text with some additions. To fill this volume, I used all of these books as resources, searched libraries, collected and borrowed pictures, and interviewed people.

I was fortunate to have the help of many people, all of whom I owe a debt of gratitude. My first thanks go to my wife and three daughters, who supported the project and sacrificed family time with me. Pete and Dorothy Hendrickson shared their memories and scrapbooks with me, as did Tracy Noon. Arthur Pearsall and I had many conversations over the past year, and he contributed his pictures and clippings. Dr. Michael Orzano and his family were more than helpful, and Maria Heller shared her resources and unending energy. Commissioner Bill Lynch, Pete O'Neill, and the Oceanside Fire Department were as generous as always. Andy Southard cared enough to stay up all night reproducing pictures for the book. Coach and historian Frank Januszewski shared many of the athletic pictures from Oceanside High School's Athletic Hall of Fame. Pam DeBaun and family, Joe and Doris Chwatsky, and Grover White all welcomed me into their homes and gave their help. Also of great help were Al and Serafina Pasetti, Roger Folz, Dr. Herb Brown, Harvey Gluck, the Messler family, the Ivarson family, Dorothy Bedell,

Mary Abel, Tom Montalbano, George Koehler, John Russell, Bob Towers, Lena Lyons, Betsy and Bob Transom, Tom Capone, Bill McCumiskey, Phil McCumiskey, Mindy Rosenthal, John Cota, Sylvia Myers, Carol Croce, Ernie Vandeweghe, Artie Wright, Frank Januszewski, Adolph Eckhardt, Jeanne Simmons, Sarah Stead Colquhoun, the Brown family, Bill Helmcke, Joe and Delores Murphy, Mr. and Mrs. Steve Buckley, the Catalanatto family, Helen Sorrentino, Steve Kriss, Eileen McCabe, Bob Baumann, Muriel Kinsman, Susan Weber, Willard Eldred, Jean Ravalli, Gladys Jacobsen, Arlene and George Parmalee, Richard Schreiber, Mike Franzini and his family, Joe Trapani, Mr. and Mrs. Emil Kuster, Joan Keefe, Ed Hynes, Barbara Schnitzer, Sheila Nigl, Mimi and Arthur Iger, Bob Patton, Phyliss Alto, Al Shea, Stuart Williams, Joan Fritzman, Marge Ghee, Thom Larsen, Gail and Bret Bennington, Howie Levy, Erin Smith, Joe Kellard, Sean Keenan, Eric Haesch, Mike D'Ambrosio, Lisa Ross, Frank Ford, Rosemary Happ, Tom DiDominica III, the Baldwin Historical Society, the Oceanside Department of Community Activities, and the librarians at the Queens Borough Public Library—Erik Huber, John Hyslop, Judith Box, and George Miller.

I hope *Oceanside* will reach many people, instill in them a sense of pride, and help them recognize the importance of their hometown and its history.

The Oceanside Triangle is one of the community's historic landmarks. Formed by three significant roads—Long Beach Road, and Lincoln and Davison Avenues—it was the site of Trolley Stop 102. The surrounding area, known as "the village," had the town's first collection of stores. Over the years the Oceanside Triangle has changed in appearance. (Courtesy of Arthur and Audrey Pearsall.)

One

NATIVE AMERICANS AND CHRISTIAN HOOK FARMERS

The land that became Oceanside and Long Island started as bedrock below the water 600 million years ago. Rivers deposited sand, gravel, and clay onto this base, building it up. Like giant bulldozers, glaciers delivered and sculpted rocks, carved the land, and left their mark on the North Shore. As the large blocks of ice melted, rivers of water carried light sediments southward to form a flat outwash plain. The South Shore was created, and Oceanside was born. (Courtesy of Andy Morris.)

The nutrient-filled sediments deposited by the glaciers made Oceanside ideal for plant life. Alongside the ponds, creeks, and dunes grew meadows, marshland, and pine trees. Pines were succeeded by oaks, chestnuts, fruit trees, and berry bushes. The marshland pictured here conjures an image of primitive Oceanside. It is a view of the Marine Nature Study Area, a 52-acre preserve that opened on Earth Day 1970. (Collection of the author.)

The fertility of the land, abundance of game, and proximity to water made Oceanside a desirable place for its first documented inhabitants, the Rockaway Indians. The Rockaways lived in single-family domed wigwams made of bark or reed. They hunted and fished in the bays. One Rockaway village known as Rechquaakie ("place of sand") was near the border of Rockville Centre and Oceanside by Shellbank Place. (Courtesy of Elisa Sabella.)

10

Unlike most tribes, the Rockaways wore their scalp feathers down. Game was abundant, but corn, beans, and squash were grown as staples. At the Oceanside–Rockville Centre border, the land that was to become the southern half of Nassau County was granted to white settlers by the Rockaway and other American Indian sachems (leaders), depicted here in a meeting with Rev. Robert Fordham, John Carmen (with axe), and John Carmen Jr. The American Indian leaders are Tackapousha, Orasguy, and Pamas. (Courtesy of Gaston Herbert.)

The Paleo-Indians had lived on Long Island for 550 generations before Henry Hudson, representing the Netherlands, arrived in the early 1600s. The Dutch saw the area as a spot where merchants could do fur trading, so they settled and occupied western Long Island and New Amsterdam (Manhattan). In 1643 the settlers arranged a successful powwow for peace with the Rockaway Indians. A celebration followed, with a feast of oysters and fish in the house of Sachem Tackapousha. Unfortunately, diseases brought by the settlers eventually wiped out two-thirds of Long Island's American Indian population. (Picture Collection, New York Public Library.)

The English settled in eastern Long Island and moved westward. On November 13, 1643, they arranged a meeting with the Rockaways to secure the land that is now southern Nassau County. The Native Americans agreed because they did not understand that anyone could own land. One signer of the document was John Carman, whose descendants settled in Oceanside. By 1650 many English were settling in Dutch areas. Peter Stuyvesant, the Dutch governor, negotiated a treaty that gave the Dutch what was to become Nassau County, and the English what was to be Suffolk. In 1664 Englishman Richard Nicolls (holding the stick) anchored warships off Long Island, and threatened to attack Fort Amsterdam; the Dutch were compelled to leave. Nicolls became the first English governor of New York state. (Picture Collection, New York Public Library.)

Long Island became part of New England, and Hempstead became the center of government. The spiritual center in Hempstead was St. George's Church (pictured), with Richard Denton as its minister. Homes were being established on the South Shore, then known as South Bay. In 1680 Denton was succeeded by Jeremiah Hobart. After Hobart ran into financial problems, the government gave him a gift of 100 acres of land near the South Bay. This property became known as the Parsonage Farm. The hook-shaped piece of land that was granted to the Christian leader gave Oceanside its first name: Christian Hook. (Collection of the author.)

This farmhouse was typical of 18th-century Christian Hook. Grain was grown and livestock was raised there. Gristmills in East Rockaway and Baldwin propelled growth. Farmers hunted for sport, and youngsters attended Huckleberry Frolics, where they picked berries by day and danced by night. Households were run with simplicity. Visiting and quilting were social events. Christian Hook was a significant community. It had a road from its southern port to Hempstead. Each fall, residents and neighbors cut the marsh grass in southern Christian Hook. They used the grass for bedding and feeding animals. Afterward, people celebrated at a festival with games, food, and drink. (Picture Collection, New York Public Library.)

13

In 1688 Joseph Haviland's East Rockaway gristmill opened on Mill River, Christian Hook's western border. On the land between Mill River and Parsonage Creek, settlers built homes and farms. Salt hay cut in southern Christian Hook was transported by cart or boat to these farms. The government controlled allotment of land; payment for the land was usually made in oats. The government also created Hempstead Commons, shared land—6,000 acres of meadow on the South Shore—on which residents could graze their animals. Since part of this commons was Christian Hook, its southern area began to be settled. Each October an event called Sheep Parting Day was held at Hempstead Commons. On that day, the sheep that grazed on the commons were separated and taken back by their individual owners. The event—which politicians used to gain votes—was a scene of rogue behavior, with gambling, drinking, and fighting. A law had to be passed that no liquor would be sold near the sheep pens after dark. (Courtesy of Queens Borough Public Library, Long Island Division.)

Two

COLONIAL TIMES
TO THE CIVIL WAR

During the 1700s the French were trying to establish territory in New York for trading, but English forces attacked them and prevailed with help from the people of Christian Hook, who aided the effort by sending sheep, cheeses, and knit goods to the English soldiers. The lessons learned readied the Colonists for the Revolutionary War. When the British taxed the Colonists to pay for their defense, many Long Islanders were resentful, but those in South Hempstead and Christian Hook remained loyal to the king. War commenced, and the rebels (depicted here) gained momentum. Some loyalists hid in the woodlands and swamps of Christian Hook. The British won the Battle of Long Island, and occupied the schoolhouse at Christian Hook. "Soldiers were [posted] for 3 or 4 miles around Hempstead. The schoolhouse at Christian Hook was occupied by some of the 60th Regiment. A half-pay officer hung himself at Parsonage [Creek]. There were Hessians [Germans fighting for Britain] at L. Cornell's Mill and at Patrick Mott's." —Henry Onderdonk, *Revolutionary Incidents on Long Island*. (Picture Collection, New York Public Library.)

From 1812 to 1814 the country was again at war with England. Depicted here are men in army and navy uniforms for the War of 1812. Citizens prepared for the worst, but Long Island was spared invasion. Col. Daniel Bedell and others organized regiments of militia for home defense. After the war, Bedell became a general. Living in Christian Hook, he worked as captain of a freighter that traveled between New York City and South Shore ports such as Mott's Landing in Christian Hook. (Picture Collection, New York Public Library.)

In 1826 James S. Pettit purchased the Parsonage Farm from St. George's Church for $2,235. It became one of the largest farms on Long Island. On the land was a farmhouse built in 1724, where Pettit's mother is thought to have grown up. This photograph shows the Pettit family burial plot on Fortesque Avenue. The remains of 10 people are buried there: seven Pettits and three with the surname Hicks. Among them is Ira Pettit, who inherited the farm from his father, James Pettit, and was mentioned in Daniel Tredwell's *Personal Reminiscences of Men and Things on Long Island* as having an "enviable reputation as a shooter." (Collection of the author.)

Christian Hook officially became a public school district in 1833. The *Long Island Farmer* newspaper stated on March 1, 1842, that the county superintendent would visit "Hempstead District #11 at Christian Hook, Thursday, April 7, 10:00 a.m." The one-room schoolhouse shown here was on the northwest corner of Oceanside and Foxhurst Roads, also known as "Jim Wright's Corner." A potbelly stove provided heat. At this time there were only 17 school districts in the town of Hempstead. Oceanside's teacher was Tony "Poppy" Waring. (Courtesy of Al Ewers.)

In the mid-1800s some Christian Hook residents converted to Mormonism. A pond near Oak Road (Fortesque Avenue) was used for full-immersion baptisms, as pictured here. The *Olean Weekly Democrat* of September 12, 1880, described it this way: "The leading Mormons are a family appropriately named Soper. The patriarch of the settlement is James Brower." Some residents traveled by horse and wagon to settle in Utah, where many of their descendants have familiar Oceanside surnames. Mormons in Oceanside held services in private dwellings. (Courtesy of Greg Schreier.)

African Americans made up as much as 25 percent of Hempstead's population in the mid-1700s. Hempstead had about 222 slaves at that time. In 1826 slavery was outlawed in New York state. From 1861 to 1865 thousands of Long Islanders served in the Civil War. Some, like the volunteer pictured above, enlisted because they felt slavery was wrong and the Union needed to be preserved. Other citizens paid for a certificate of exemption. And other Long Island natives were drafted. The September 3, 1863 *New York Times* listed six residents of Christian Hook who had been drafted: E. Denton, A. Soper, B. Miller, G. Smith, W. Story, and A. S. Jones. The September 1, 1864 *Queens County Sentinel* recorded that Christian Hook natives John Eldred, Elbert Pettit, and Alexander Rhodes had been conscripted. Among other locals who served were Martin Van Buren Murray, John H. Anthony, and Charles Phillips. Phillips, who was a bodyguard for Lincoln at Gettysburg, died in Oceanside at the home of his daughter, Mrs. Frank Seaman, on February 22, 1932. (Picture Collection, New York Public Library.)

Three

OYSTERS AND
RURAL OCEANVILLE

The oyster industry epitomizes Christian Hook during the last half of the 19th century, as noted in *A History of Queens County:* "The oyster industry began about 1860, and has become very profitable in Freeport, Christian Hook and East Rockaway." Thousands of barrels were shipped each season to New York City, where scenes like this one of an oyster cart and a man sampling the goods, were common. Oysters from Christian Hook were of premium quality. Mott's Landing, at the neck of southern Christian Hook, became a fast-growing section of the community. The *South Side Observer* of May 23, 1890, wrote, "Mott's Dock was for many years known as Jim Smith's Landing. . . . With the commodious residences of Capt. W. H. Mott, surrounded by its well-kept grounds and the number of neat cottages, . . . this landing presents an attractive appearance. . . ." It was also noted that William H. Mott was the "largest shipper of oysters on the south side." At the "landing" were Mott's General Store and bay houses where oysters were shucked. (Picture Collection, New York Public Library.)

Oysters were taken by wagon up Christian Hook Road (now Oceanside Road) to Merrick and Jamaica Plank Road (Merrick Road), where they were transported to the city. In 1864 Christian Hook became Oceanville because people felt it would be easier to sell oysters if the community's name had a nautical ring. Oceanville baymen—unique, tough, and independent—were tagged with the nickname "clam diggers." They lived in houses like the one shown here. (Collection of the author.)

Oceanside's original street, Silver Lane, is said to have been named for the oyster shells that lined its path and emitted a silver shine in the daytime sun. This house on Silver Lane was owned by Abraham Combs and was built c. 1863. Behind it was an asparagus farm, which bordered the property of Robert B. Roosevelt, cousin of Teddy Roosevelt. Abraham Combs and Teddy Roosevelt were friends and spent time together in this house. (Collection of the author.)

On October 28, 1867, the South Side Railroad of Long Island opened a line from Jamaica, Queens, to Babylon, along the south "side" of Long Island. The train ran just north of Oceanville, and stopped in an area known as "the pine barrens" (Rockville Centre). The stop before Rockville Centre was Pearsalls (now Lynbrook), and the stop after was Baldwins (Baldwin). The train provided an easier and faster way for Oceanville farmers and baymen to transport goods to New York City, but it also meant a change in the status quo. With the advent of the train line, newcomers and real estate promoters abounded. "Foreigners" who moved in were looked upon with suspicion by the old community families, who in turn were viewed by the new residents as country bumpkins. (Courtesy of Ron Ziel.)

FIRST PRESBYTERIAN CHURCH,
OCEANSIDE, LONG ISLAND, N. Y.

On Sundays, people in Christian Hook traveled to the Presbyterian churches in Hempstead or Freeport. In 1848, with support from these churches, Maria Pine started a Sunday school in the schoolhouse. In 1868 Rev. Marcus Burr began holding services there, and became the church's first pastor. In 1871 a church building was constructed diagonally across from the school. Shown here is that church, which was founded on October 31, 1871, with 10 members. (Courtesy of the Oceanside Presbyterian Church.)

Land for the church building was donated by Townsend Southard, who had a farm at that location. He is seen here in an 1890 photograph. The church became the central location for community gatherings—dances, meetings, and social activities—as well as worship. Each fall the congregation held a community dinner and fair at which farmers sold produce, with proceeds going to support the church. In the spring the church held a strawberry festival at Soper's Grove. (Courtesy of Andy Southard Jr.)

Away from the bays, Oceanville was an area with scattered family farms. Farm families raised their own food, fed their cows with homegrown forage, and used hired help only in the busy season. Surplus was carried by horse and wagon to the Brooklyn market. Unlike the baymen who used "modern" Christian Hook Road, farmers traveled dirt paths to get to Merrick and Jamaica Plank Road. Farmers and baymen had to pay a toll in Valley Stream, Jamaica, and East New York. Seen here is Wettach Farm, owned by real estate entrepreneur Anton Wettach (far left). The men are standing where the Oceanside High School soccer field is today. Behind them is Skillman Avenue. (Courtesy of Carol Croce.)

East Rockaway

R. Johnson

Mrs. Wood

J. Driscoll

A. Demott

J. B

C. Brackett

Davison Bros.

Avenue

E. Burley

Dan'l Pearsall

Wm. Rhodes

A. Pearsall

Mrs. Davison

J. Sho

Mrs. A. Longdon

Anthony DeMott

Mrs. A. Longdon

V. Smith

J. Watts

J. Lamberton

P. Shay

J. Wood Sr.

Geo. Willis

Oliver Langdon

Store

Jas. Combs

H. Huits

Dan'l Terrell

V. Combs

M. Murray

N. Pearsall

F. Wright

Thos. Foster

J. H. Watts

E. Southard

J. Boyd

L. Abra

W. Wright

Joe McCann

Able Wood

Hans Stillive

A. Combs

Rockaway

R. W. Poole

R. W. Poole

J. Denton Shop

W. Davison

C. Driscoll

J. Saxon

A. Driscoll

R. Roosevelt

N. Terrell

W. Ackerly

N. Smith

Store House

Lumber Yard

S. Combs

Bedell Store

S. Rider

Carriage Shop

Blacksmith

Powells Creek

W. Davison

W. Clemens

Q. Wood

G. H. Smith

Geo. Davison

W. Soper

W. Poole

D. Ousterman

M. Wood

Smith's Store

E. Smith

H. Davison

J. Wood

S. Soper

S. Simonson

S. Wright

J. Pearsall

E. Soper

T. So

Mrs. Story

L. Hewlett

Pettit's Store

S. Ousterman

A. Cornwell

A. Cornwell

D. & B. De Mott

Springs Tr

J. Bedell

J. Smith

W. Rhodes

G. Rhodes

W. Doxy

Dr. Webb

E. Hultz

B. Shore

W. Rhode

A. Noon

Map showing the District known as ~

Oceanside,
Long Island

as it was in 1870
showing each house and the owner's name thereof
Approximate Scale

0   ½ Mi.

Done from old & musty records by the Nelson Studio, St. James, N.Y.

24

The map labels include:

J. Mount
E. Hultz
ison
Frost W. Griffin
Wm. Smith Chas. Cornell
E. Seaman
W.P. Soper
H. Soper
k Smith
J. Fox
M. Story
J. Story
J. Fox
G. Soper
sall
ettit
W.J. Bond
J. Brower, Sr.
on Est.
J. Brower, Jr.
Mrs. Smith
C. Pettit
I. Pettit
S. Wood

N
W
E
S

taker

Hempstead
Bay

This map of Christian Hook c. 1870 shows the major streets, the homes, and the names of the homeowners. Note the many homes on Silver Lane, east of Rockaway Avenue. The Silver Lane–Atlantic Avenue–Rockaway Avenue region was Oceanside's first neighborhood. There, people had everything they needed—farmland, access to roads and water, Davison's Lumber Yard, and a general store. The Presbyterian church and some of the homes shown here are still standing. Others, including the original schoolhouse, blacksmith shops, general stores, and carriage shops, are long gone. The southern area of Christian Hook was unpopulated because of its spongy marshland. (Courtesy of Frank Januszewski.)

T. G. KNIGHT,

—BREEDER OF—

REGISTERED JERSEY CATTLE,

Oakwood Park, Oceanville.

—o—

To encourage an interest in Jersey Cattle in our vicinity and afford those desirous of improving their stock, an opportunity of securing the services of a splendid BUTTER Bull, g. s. of DUKE OF DAR-LINGTON, whose dam EUROTAS made 22 lbs. 7 oz. in one week and 778 lbs. butter in one year, and whose daughter BOMBA made 21 lbs. 11½ oz. in one week,

Florindes Duke 3rd, No. 7028,

A. J. C. C. Herd Register, will stand at my Farm at OCEANVILLE. Service Fee—Registered Cows, $25, all other cows, $5. In all cases cash in advance, and cows not proving can be returned free.

T. G. KNIGHT,

8t-955   P. O. Box 10, Rockville Centre, L. I.

Oceanville farmers were tenacious and enterprising. The *New York Times* of April 2, 1887, reported that Elbert Seaman got a posse of farmers armed with pitchforks to stop the Rockaway Hunt Club from trampling their fields as they had done the previous year during their fox hunt. Thomas Knight brought Long Island its first Jersey cows, which he bred and sold. The price of a Jersey calf was $200 to $400. Knight's farm was south of Brower Avenue, and included the location of present-day Knight Street. Seen at left is Thomas Knight's newspaper ad of May 23, 1883. (*South Side Observer.*)

In 1873 Oceanville had about 200 landowners, most of whom were farmers. *A History of Queens County* offers this description of Christian Hook–Oceanville in 1882: "Among the principal farmers and residents are the Pettits, Sopers, Joseph Brower, Z. Story and the Conways. Since 1826, Ira Pettit has lived on his present farm, a fine one, commanding a beautiful view seaward." In the fall, farmers would prepare for the Mineola Fair. In 1882 Edward Seaman brought two 900-pound hogs, and Franklin Soper brought his two-year-old stallion, Forrest Hunter Jr. Seen here is the Mineola Fair in 1910. (Collection of the author.)

On the northeast corner of Christian Hook Road and School Street stood Lorenzo Davison's General Store. Lorenzo's father, George, was a Christian Hook farmer. Lorenzo sold guns, flour, yarn, oil, wood, coal, and school supplies. His duck and poultry farm was next to the store, and across the street were his coal yard and blacksmith shop. The general store was the place where great issues were debated, from the price of oysters to who should be elected president. Each spring, Mary Pettit would open up an ice-cream tent next to the store. (Courtesy of the Baldwin Historical Society.)

In 1880, with approximately 300 families living in Oceanville, a new school was needed. Shown here are students and school staff in front of that new schoolhouse in 1888. From left to right are the following: (first row) Jennie Raynor, Vivian Rorer, Stella Brower, Emily Ramsden, Mamie Rider, Rosie Story, Kate Combs, Maggie Davison, Lillie Smith, Lizzie Seaman, Susie Terrell, Ada Combs, Grace Smith, Jennie Johnson, and Alice Johnson; (second row) Will Raynor, Gilbert Smith, Joe Mount, Lew Helmker, Edgar Davison, Henry Raynor, Oscar Terrell, Mr. Williams (principal), Miss Tate (teacher), Gertie Grady, Carrie Combs, Ada Hill, Libbie Southard, and Goldie Newall. (Courtesy of Pete and Dorothy Hendrickson.)

Oceanville was populated primarily by baymen and farmers. The skill of the blacksmith, who shaped iron into tools, was crucial. The blacksmith created and repaired farm and bay implements, shod horses, and made firearms. Above the clinking of the hammer and anvil, gossip was exchanged and political issues were discussed. Pictured is Warren Abrams, who had a shop on Merle Avenue. Another blacksmith shop owned by William Rhodes operated from 1881 to 1933 on Long Beach Road at Fairview Avenue. (Courtesy of Joe Chwatsky.)

New Millinery !

A Large Stock Just Re eived. HATS trimmed to order on short notice, at

MRS, RYDER'S STORE, Oceanville.

Also a Fine Stock of GROCERIES. FLOUR very LOW by the Barrel.   3t-61

In Phoebe Ryder's store, people would say, "You could buy everything there but coffins." In December 1884 Ryder's store, which stood on the corner of what is now Davison Avenue and Oceanside Road, was robbed by three "tramps." Franklin Noon found the stolen loot. To gain notoriety, he fabricated a tale that the location of the money had been revealed to him in a dream. Noon then told police he had also dreamed that the thieves were at Barnum's Island. Subsequently, three men were arrested at the island, and Noon received a $150 reward. During the trio's court case it became clear that Noon's dream had been just that, and the accused men were released. (*South Side Observer*.)

Four

THE EARLY 1900S

In 1889 Oceanville applied for a post office. Lorenzo Davison was to serve as the town's postmaster. Since the name "Oceanville" was already in use for two other post offices, the community's name was changed to Ocean Side. A local newspaper reported: "The establishment of a post office is another step in the march of progress for Christian Hook, or Oceanville, or Ocean Side. The latter is a good name, and after the office is 'running' a while it is likely that Ocean Side will be the name of the place." The post office opened on November 2, 1892. Davison was also the local fire dispatcher in the early 1900s. In this photograph, the sign hanging below the L. DAVISON sign reads "POST OFFICE." The boys next to the tree on the left are brothers Andy and Townsend Lee Southard. Andy became the receiver of taxes for the town of Hempstead. He was also a school board member, and was active in local civic affairs. (Courtesy of Joe Trapani.)

In 1895 the school building was sold to Philip Martiny, who moved it to Terrell Avenue. Martiny, a renowned sculptor, created many of his great works there. His work adorns New York City, where his baby-like winged cherub, seen in this photograph, has graced the entrance of Manhattan's Herald Square Hotel for over 100 years. In the Jefferson Building of the Library of Congress in Washington, D.C., the two staircases flanking the Great Hall are embellished by Martiny's sculptural work. (Collection of the author.)

Oceansiders who wished to be part of a Methodist congregation worshiped at the Bethel Church in Baldwin, the Sand Hole Church in Lynbrook, and later St. Mark's Church in Rockville Centre. In 1895 services led by Rev. Joe McCoun were held above George Wood's Store on the corner of Nassau Road and Atlantic Avenue. Eventually, a plot on the corner of Atlantic Avenue and Davison Street was bought from William Davison. The church building was completed in 1896. The first full-time pastor of the church was Rev. R. Stanley Povey. (Collection of the author.)

New York City gradually began taking over western Long Island. In 1898 Hempstead, North Hempstead, and Oyster Bay, wishing to avoid becoming part of New York City, proposed a new county, and on January 1, 1899, Nassau County was created. The lion on its coat of arms, seen here, signifies ferocity, bravery, and wisdom. Ocean Side has an inauspicious distinction as the site of the county's first murder: Samuel Ousterman killed Thomas Nickerson there in April 1899. Nickerson and a friend had stopped to pay a visit to Ousterman's maid, but Ousterman objected. The two men left, but not before throwing beer bottles through Ousterman's windows. Ousterman then issued an ultimatum, which the two callers did not heed. (Courtesy of the Town of Hempstead.)

According to the book *New York and Long Island Traction Company*, in 1895 a push to develop north-south transit came from owners of large estates in Ocean Side and Long Beach. On September 21, 1903, the trolley began rolling through Ocean Side. It ran from Jamaica to Hempstead, and had nine stops in Ocean Side on Woods Avenue, Davison Avenue, and Brower Avenue. Ocean Side's most famous stop was No. 102, known today as "the Triangle." (Courtesy of Grover White.)

Shown here are the trolley tracks running between the unpaved street and the sidewalks of Woods Avenue. The shot looks toward Davison Avenue. To the right is the back of Columbia Firehouse; to the left is a cigar store (now a karate school). The flagpole marks the triangle. Behind it is a house with a sign that says "Restaurant." (Courtesy of the Queens Borough Public Library, Long Island Division.)

Oceanside's business was centered around Trolley Stop No. 102 on Davison Avenue, where dirt crossroads, Long Beach Road and Lincoln Avenue formed a triangle. This was the site of a collection of stores, and Ocean Siders who were going shopping might say, "I'm going to pick up some things at 102." This postcard shows the triangle looking south down Long Beach Road. The barely legible sign on the white pole says "Oceanside." (Collection of the author.)

Looking southward in 1915, this picture of the triangle shows a real estate office on the right, with Henry Reithermann's grocery, fruit, vegetable, and tobacco shop next door. The Columbia Firehouse is in the right background. The pole on the triangle to the right warns pedestrians about the trolley; the pole to the left carries a sign that says "Oceanside." At the back left is a chicken farm; seen on the dirt roads is horse manure. (Courtesy of the Queens Borough Public Library, Long Island Division.)

The surname Pearsall is a significant one in Oceanside. The Pearsalls, who arrived in 1635, were among the earliest families on Long Island. Lynbrook, founded by the family, was originally called Pearsalls. The name can be found—both past and present—in education, business, fishing, farming, the fire department, and every other sector of life in Oceanside. Shown here are, from left to right, Melissa Pearsall, Lila Pearsall (née Combs), Audrey Pearsall (holding Russell Pearsall), and Stella Pearsall. (Courtesy of Arthur and Audrey Pearsall.)

As Oceanside became a vacation spot, hotels were needed. The Oaks Inn (above and below), was erected south of Brower Avenue, near Parsonage Creek, during the summer of 1900. The neighborhood known as The Oaks bordered on Parsonage Creek, from Brower Avenue to Foxhurst Road, and the area around Fortesque Avenue. Fortesque was named Oak Road at the time; School No. 3 is still known as Oaks School No. 3. The Oaks Inn, easily reached by water, had a bar and was a place where men could meet "working women." The hotel burned down c. 1916. (Courtesy of Arthur and Audrey Pearsall.)

In June 1903 Oceanside held its first high school commencement. The graduating class had just two members, Bertha Pettit and Julia Shea. At the time, the school offered only a two-year program. The two graduates had to complete the work needed for a Regents Diploma by continuing their education in the Rockville Centre School District. The first graduation ceremony for four-year students was held in 1907. That year, the valedictorian was Mabel Peace—who was also the only graduate. This photograph shows the first high school building, constructed in 1911. (Courtesy of Grover White.)

The new school building cost $75,000, and accommodated 400 grammar school students and 50 high schoolers. The first high school commencement ceremony was held in an unfinished third floor. Because of a power outage, the ceremony was lit by gas lanterns. The old school building (seen above) was sold to John Terrell. He moved the structure to Davison Avenue, where it became a place for parties, meetings, and religious services. "Terrell Hall" was torn down in 1972. (Courtesy of Maria Heller.)

State Sen. John Fox, who lived in Ocean Side, was a delegate to the Democratic National Convention in 1876, 1904, and 1912. His property, just north of The Oaks, extended further north, where it straddled School Street. Fox dubbed his mansion and beautiful estate Foxhurst, and School Street eventually became Foxhurst Road. This photograph shows where Foxhurst Road and Grand Avenue meet. The road to the right goes to Ocean Side. The horse and wagon could be the senator's. (Courtesy of the Baldwin Historical Society.)

On March 1, 1902, a group of 20 men met at the home of Thomas T. Ramsden to organize a fire company in Ocean Side. The meeting was prompted by a fire that had destroyed the Pettit farmhouse. Ramsden suggested the name Salamander for the fire company (a salamander is not only a lizard but also a mythical creature that can endure fire without harm). On January 26, 1903, the members voted to purchase a truck for $368. In 1905 Mary Bennett donated land on School Street for the fire hall (on the left). The members constructed the two-story building. (Courtesy of Richard Schreiber.)

This 1907 photograph is an eastward view of School Street (Foxhurst Road). The belfry of Salamander Firehouse is visible between the telephone poles. The pole across the top of the tree-lined street was used for firefighting exercises. Note the couple in the horse and buggy and the bicyclist in her long dress. (Courtesy of Grover White.)

William D. Southard lived on Merle Avenue. Here he is seen out for a ride, with his dog on his lap. (Courtesy of Andy Southard Jr.)

In the fall of 1902 Columbia Engine Company was organized. Sanford Davison applied for a charter on November 1, 1902. Meetings were held at George Wood's Hall on Atlantic Avenue and Nassau Road. Members purchased a double-tank chemical engine that could either be drawn by horse or by hand. On May 11, 1905, the Poole family donated land on the southwest corner of Lincoln and Davison Avenues for the erection of the building shown here, which still stands. Its upper floor was a site for meetings and social functions. (Courtesy of Pete O'Neill.)

Hose Company No. 1, the community's third firehouse, served northwest Ocean Side. It was chartered by the state of New York on April 6, 1906. As with Columbia, meetings were originally held at George Wood's Hall. The company's first elected officers were Charles Kuster, foreman, and George J. Simonson, assistant foreman. John F. Kruger (pictured) was an original trustee. A truck and hose was purchased a year later, and was housed in the wagon shed at the Methodist church. (Courtesy of the Brown family.)

In 1880 a railroad line ran from Lynbrook to Long Beach, a new seaside resort and site of the famous Long Beach Hotel. The train ran through Ocean Side but did not make stops there until 1906, when a stop was created at Ocean Side. This was an early step toward the making of a New York City suburb. *Out on the Island,* a railroad promotional booklet, described Oceanside as "a contiguous settlement, over 20 of which are occupied by retired 'Down-East' shipmasters." Shown here is the waiting station. (Courtesy of Ron Ziel.)

39

While the railroad stop was being created in Oceanside, a drawbridge was built so that boat traffic could continue through Powell's Creek. The creek veers off the East Rockaway Channel and continues under the train tracks across Lawson Boulevard. It then moves along Bayside Avenue and Terrell Avenue, and across Woods Avenue to Rockville Centre. The creek no longer has boat traffic, but it does contain snapping turtles and other wildlife. Shown here is the construction of the Powell's Creek drawbridge in 1906. (Courtesy of the Queens Borough Public Library, Long Island Division.)

This 1914 map shows a few of the names of Ocean Side's neighborhoods. Western Ocean Side between Atlantic and Bayside Avenues was known as Bungalow Park. The area around School No. 2 was Willard Park; just north, straddling Ocean Side and Rockville Centre, was Woodland Park. Between Nassau Road and Lincoln Avenue was Bayview Park; south of Bayview Park was Oceanside Park and, farther south, the Meadows. Shown here are the Woodlawn Park and Fairview Park areas. (Courtesy of Arlene and George Parmalee.)

In the early 1900s, silent movies were made in Phillip Martiny's house on Terrell Avenue by a company called Ocean Film Corporation. The company made three pictures between 1915 and 1916. One of them, *Life Without a Soul*, was loosely based on Mary Shelley's *Frankenstein*. According to Anthony Slide's *The American Film Industry*, Harry R. Raver of Rockville Centre took over the company in 1916. In 1917 Oceanside's Grace Davison (pictured) made her film debut in *Hell Hath No Fury*. She did her own stunts. Some of Davison's films were shot in Freeport and East Rockaway, and she eventually started her own movie company, J. G. Productions. Davison married Hollis Hughes, a widely recognized breeder of thoroughbred horses. On their wedding day, the couple surprised guests by dressing up two monkeys as a bride and groom and letting them loose before the ceremony. (Corbis Stock Photography.)

The Boy Scouts of America started in 1910, and two years later produced their first Eagle Scout, Arthur Eldred, from Oceanside's Troop No. 1, the first troop on the South Shore of Nassau County. This photograph shows Eldred in uniform in front of his Terrell Avenue home. He obtained his badge on Labor Day 1912. A few weeks later, Eldred helped save another Scout from drowning and received a bronze medal for his feat. He graduated from Oceanside High School in 1912, and was the first graduate to receive a Regents Certificate. (Courtesy of Willard Eldred.)

As the United States entered World War I, so did Oceanside residents Claude Noon and Wilbur A. Cornell, who fought in France. Two who died in the war were Edwin Abrams and Francesco Molisse. Mary Rogers (pictured) enlisted and performed clerical work for the U.S. Naval Reserves in New York City. She came to Oceanside in the 1940s, taught religious education classes at St. Anthony's, and volunteered for many causes. When she died, she had 3 children and 15 grandchildren living in Oceanside. (Courtesy of Joan Woods.)

Five

GROWTH IN THE 1920S

In the 1920s people of wealth lived alongside people of modest means in Oceanside. One wealthy, famous person who had an estate in Oceanside was dancer Gilda Gray. Born in Poland, she came to this country with her family to escape the Russians. Gray's signature dance was the "shimmy"—there was a time when no one on Broadway could get a dancing job unless she could shimmy like Gilda Gray. The dance was born one night when Gray was trying to sing "The Star-Spangled Banner" and, while struggling to pronounce the words, she wiggled as if to compensate for her lack of skill in English. When asked what she was doing, she said, "Shaking my shimmy" (her pronunciation of *chemise*)." (Collection of the author.)

When Gilda Gray arrived in New York City, she danced in the Ziegfield Follies. After Gray had divorced her first husband and married Gaillard T. Boag, they bought the house in Oceanside. (Its shingles had his monogram, "GTB," carved into them.) Gray's luck changed at the end of the 1920s with the stock market crash. In the spring of 1933 she sold her house to Earl Towers. She was known to have given money to Oceanside butcher Emil Janowski so that he could give food to the poor. Gray was no recluse—she would shimmy when a fan asked her to. This photograph is from *The Devil Dancer* (1927). (Collection of the author.)

In the 1920s one place to shop for food was the Oceanside Meat Market on the corner of Woods Avenue and Davis Street. It was owned by George Koller (seen behind the counter), who was known for his generosity, especially during the Depression. Families paid on credit, and frequently their debts would be erased. (Courtesy of Mr. and Mrs. Emil Kuster.)

Windsor Parkway, Ocean Side, L. I.

This picture, looking east, shows Windsor Parkway as a wide dirt road. Local resident Tracy Noon remembers horse races being held in this block before the street was paved. Trotters with jockeys in sulkies provided entertainment for the locals. The jockeys were Jake Belford, and Nelson and Gene Abrams. (Courtesy of Erich Haesche.)

In January 1920—with a population increase to about 1,800 causing crowded conditions—the Oceanside Board of Education brought to the taxpayers a proposition to build a new grammar school. The site chosen was four parcels of land at Terrell Avenue. The building was completed in the fall of 1922. Shown here is a School No. 2 sixth-grade class. Pictured are, from left to right, the following: (first row) Gerald Hammel (standing), Adele Gilks, June Lacey, May Wood, Gloria Gottleib, and Myrtle Von Volkenberg; (second row) Roy Mohler (standing), Miss Nunnenkampf, Mary Mehan, Tina Tafuri, Vivian Yellon, Anne Mc Grath, Clare Keegan, Helen Klosterman, and Eileen Bonner; (third row) Henry Peterson, unidentified, Alvin Knox, two unidentified persons, Everett Baylis, Perry Brockett, Naomi Whitehouse, Edna Terrell, unidentified, and Gertrude Hewitt; (fourth row) Bob McFadden, Paul Gritman, Dave Graves, Pete Hendrickson, Arthur Johnson, and Katherine Johnson. (Courtesy of Pete and Dorothy Hendrickson.)

45

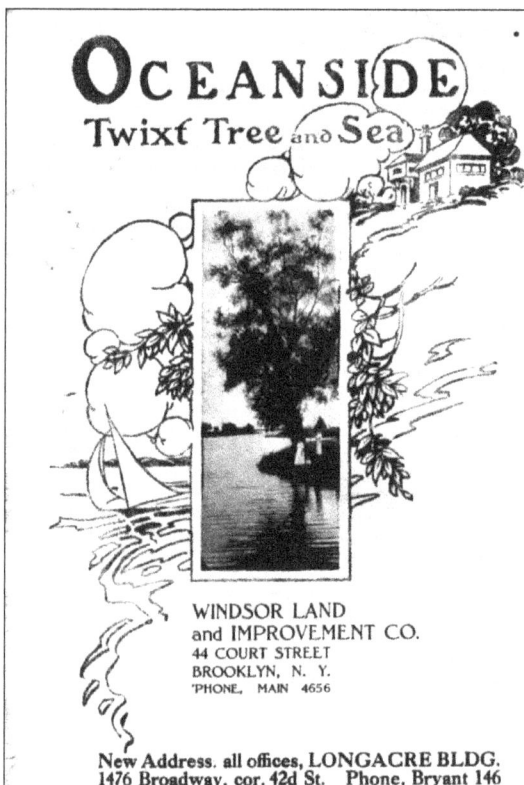

In the 1920s real estate companies like the Windsor Land and Improvement Company were selling property to build new homes. People of wealth were beginning to settle in Oceanside. The Windsor brochure advertises Oceanside as rural, with the advantages of being near the ocean. Note that *Oceanside* is spelled here as one word. Some people attribute this change to a trend among all the Long Island towns to consolidate their two-word names. Others claim that it was the school principal, S. Taylor Johnson, who started writing the community's name as one word. (Courtesy of Richard Schreiber.)

The inside of the Windsor brochure promotes all that is good about Oceanside in 1928. Lots sold for as little as $10 down. Entrepreneurs would rent a railroad car and pile in passengers from New York City. Once they arrived, the visitors were treated to beer and food. Trips were offered for individual ethnic groups: Italian, Jewish, Polish, Irish—each had their day. Many of those who bought land in the 1920s lost their property during the Depression because they could not pay the taxes. (Courtesy of Richard Schreiber.)

William Kennelly held auctions for the sale of many Oceanside properties in the 1920s. From a Kennelly real estate prospectus, this scene, looking east, shows Foxhurst Road a short distance from Oceanside Road. The area was advertised as Foxhurst Park, and Oceanside was touted as the first woods and country, this side of Long Beach, where a cellar could be dug. The two houses shown in the brochure are still there (the car is probably long gone). (Courtesy of Richard Schreiber.)

AUCTION SALE
Oceanside, *Long Island* Properties

Including Admirably Located

HOUSES AND BUNGALOWS, BUSINESS AND RESIDENTIAL LOTS
in Oceanside, Foxhurst Park, Skillman Gardens, Miramar, Oceanside, L. I. and Kings' Estate, Baldwin. *Also*

UNRESTRICTED

85 Business and Residential LOTS
in "OCEANSIDE ESTATES"

Oceanside Parkway, and Brower Avenue are Improved with Water, Gas, Electricity, Sidewalks, Curbs and Paved Streets

SATURDAY, SEPTEMBER 29

1928, at 2 o'Clock P. M., rain or shine, under large tent located at

Junction of Oceanside Road, Davison and Brower Avenues

WILLIAM KENNELLY, Real Estate Auctioneers
INCORPORATED

| 149 BROADWAY | Telephone: Hanover 1020 | NEW YORK CITY |

This advertisement, put out by William Kennelly for his auction sale of Oceanside lots, lists the names of local neighborhoods. Most of these names are not used today. Features now taken for granted, such as paved streets and electricity, were selling points in 1928. (Courtesy of Richard Schreiber.)

47

In the 1920s an improvement project was undertaken on the shores of the East Rockaway Inlet, on the southwestern side of Oceanside. The result was an increase in the amount of goods imported and exported by ship. The project was facilitated by a government appropriation. Credit was given to Edward J. Hughes, a Mineola trustee. The docks at "Oceanside Terminal" received building materials, produce, and fuel oil. Hughes said of the project: "Marshlands have been transformed into a bee-hive of activity. . . . Oceanside is destined for big things. It will soon be the industrial hub of Nassau County." The area, as seen here, is still used today; it is the site of many oil holding tanks and is nicknamed Oil City.

On the corner of Foxhurst and Oceanside Roads, the former site of Davison's General Store, in the 1920s stood the Yankee Service Station, owned by the Catalanatto family. The building's structure had not changed much, but the products had. This service station doubled as a call station for the fire department. The Catalanattos were firefighters, and Lou Catalanatto had a barbershop across the street. The corner is occupied today by Island Auto Body. (Courtesy of the Catalanatto family.)

On May 27, 1921, the school burned. As seen here, the building was gutted, but the brick structure remained unscarred. Principal S. Taylor Johnson ran in during the fire to recover school records, but he had to retreat. Afterward, students were divided into groups to continue their education at churches, fire halls, and barns. After Thanksgiving 1922, most of the students were housed in the new Terrell Avenue School No. 2. In September 1923 a new fireproof building was erected on the same site as the old school. (Courtesy of Grover White.)

In 1921 a business opened up on Long Beach Road to serve the needs of travelers passing through Oceanside en route to Long Beach. The owners, Leon Shor and Murray Hadfield, called their tiny fruit and vegetable stand the Roadside Rest. Resident Tracy Noon swears that they stole vegetables from his father's farm on Roosevelt Street. Baldwin resident Grover White says that his uncle, Jake Pettit, a motorcycle policeman at the time, gave Shor and Hadfield permission to set up shop there. (Collection of the author.)

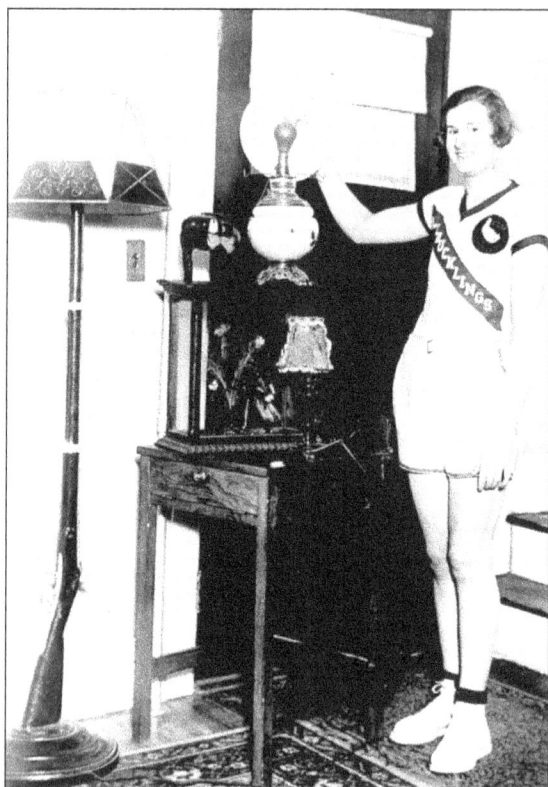

One of Oceanside's greatest athletes and personalities in the 1920s was Melissa Pearsall. During her high school years, she dominated in athletic competition; in basketball, she was the highest scorer in Nassau County. Later Pearsall played basketball for the Long Island Ducklings, and pitched for the New York Bloomer Girls. Pearsall was also a carpenter, painter, mechanic, and plumber. She was a member of the Veterans of Foreign Wars and was dedicated to caring for veterans. At the age of 92, "Aunt Mel" still lives in Oceanside. This photograph shows her in her Ducklings uniform showing off some things she made in high school shop class. (Courtesy of Arthur and Audrey Pearsall.)

Another noted personality living in Oceanside during the 1920s was Broadway performer Frank Tinney. He lived on Foxhurst Road at the former residence of Sen. John Fox. The area around his house was referred to as Tinney's Woods. Baldwin resident Adolph Eckhardt said that Tinney kept several horses and other animals there, and also entertained many stars, including Will Rogers. On July 4, 1927, the *New York Times* reported that Tinney's Oceanside home had burned down. In his last days, Tinney lived in Northport. (Courtesy of Grover White.)

The southern waters of Oceanside abound with scallops, oysters, clams, and eels. Throughout Oceanside's history, hunting and fishing were pursued for sport, for sustenance, or as a means of making a living. From the town's earliest days through the early 1900s, the bay was a source of income. Baymen developed their own unique dialect and customs. This photograph represents Oceanside's version of the painting *American Gothic*. The husband-and-wife team are Emily and Wesley Tredwell. Emily is holding an eel spear; Wesley holds a fish. (Courtesy of Emily Tredwell.)

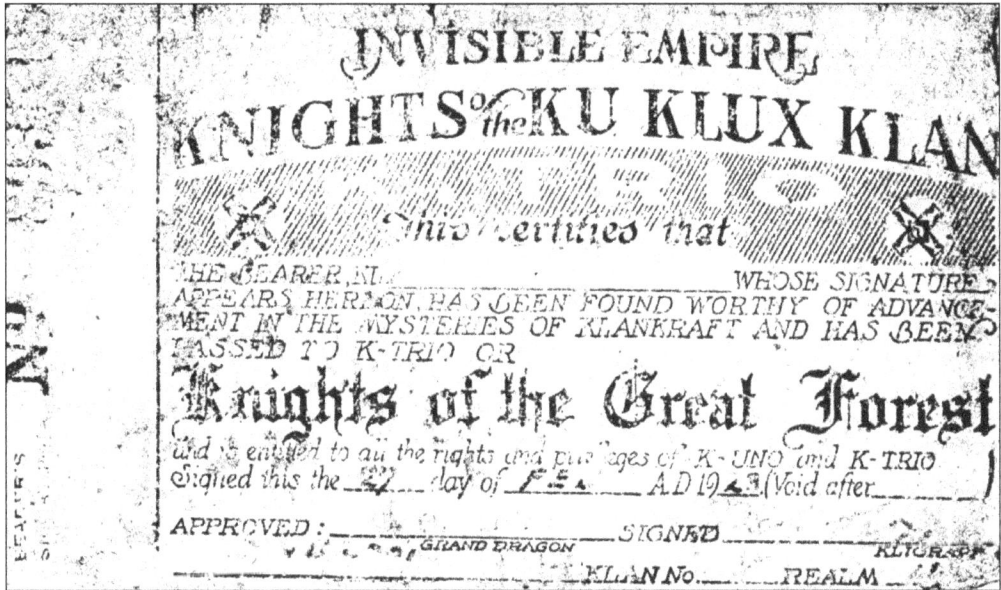

INVISIBLE EMPIRE

KNIGHTS of the KU KLUX KLAN

This certifies that

THE BEARER, NL_____ WHOSE SIGNATURE APPEARS HEREON, HAS BEEN FOUND WORTHY OF ADVANCE- MENT IN THE MYSTERIES OF KLANKRAFT AND HAS BEEN PASSED TO K-TRIO OR

Knights of the Great Forest

and is entitled to all the rights and privileges of K-UNO and K-TRIO Signed this the ___ day of ___ A.D. 19__(Void after_____)

APPROVED :_____ SIGNED_____
GRAND DRAGON   KLIGRAPP
_____ KLAN No._____ REALM _____

Older residents of Oceanside remember the local Ku Klux Klan, and some had relatives who were Klan members. On July 25, 1925, the *New York Times* reported a 10,000-person KKK "karnival" and parade were held in Oceanside. The parade marched to a field on Oceanside Road, where people were entertained with a rodeo and vaudeville program. When darkness fell, a 40-foot cross was burned. The Klan resented people who were foreign-born, African American, Catholic, or Jewish. After Oceanside's first Catholic Church was completed, several crosses were burned in front of it. The card shown here, from 1923, is from an Oceanside Klansman.

In 1925 the State Department of Education recommended that Oceanside consider hiring a superintendent to guide its growing school district. Supervising principal S. Taylor Johnson was appointed to that position. In 1926 it became apparent that more school space was needed, and the school board agreed to build two elementary schools, No. 3 and No. 4. School No. 3 was opened on September 26, 1926, and School No. 4 was opened the following February. Shown here is No. 3. (Courtesy of Richard Schreiber.)

To stop the loss of local banking business to other communities, Oceanside businessmen applied for a federal bank charter in 1923, and in November of that year the Oceanside National Bank opened its first offices in a small store, with Rufus H. Smith as its first president. By 1928 the bank had grown, and the incorporators financed the construction of a building on the corner of Poole Street and Lincoln Avenue, where it remains today. (Courtesy of the *Oceanside Annual*.)

Rufus Smith played a great role in moving Oceanside forward during the 1920s. After his father was murdered by clam poachers while he was guarding the waters one night, Smith's mother, Adella Smith (born in Christian Hook in 1854), continued to raise her 10-year-old son and his two siblings. Rufus Smith worked on the family farm, graduated from New York University Law School, and thereafter began a successful career in real estate. Smith was a trustee at the First Presbyterian Church for over 30 years. He served as a delegate to a national convention at Saratoga at the time when his friend Theodore Roosevelt was president of that delegation. Smith used his wealth to do enormous good: he founded Oceanside National Bank, donated land to St. Anthony's Shrine, and gave money to start South Nassau Communities Hospital. He could broker a fair deal better than anyone, and was known for giving a loan based on a person's word. In this photograph, Rufus Smith (center) sits in the company of his family. With him are, from left to right, granddaughter Diane Vandeweghe, daughter Mary (Smith) Vandeweghe, mother Adella Smith, and grandson Ernest Vandeweghe. (Courtesy of Diane Scalamandre.)

The third church established in Oceanside was St. Andrew's Episcopal Church. The first service was held September 26, 1926, in Columbia Fire Hall. Mrs. Alexander A. Pearsall, wife of the famous oysterman, donated a site on Anchor Avenue for the church. On September 11, 1927, the church building was dedicated. Its first minister was Frederick H. Handsfield. (Collection of the author.)

Fr. Robert Barrett was born in Ireland and came to the United States in 1920. He had assignments of pastorship in Brooklyn and Great Neck before he arrived in Oceanside in 1927. Barrett was a character with a strong, gregarious personality. He celebrated the first Mass in Oceanside at the Salamander Firehouse on May 15, 1927, for 14 people. His foremost goal was the construction of a church. The land north of Windsor Parkway and east of Lincoln Avenue became the site of Barrett's new church. He was the architect of the beautiful shrine church, St. Anthony's, which became one of the biggest tourist attractions on Long Island. (Courtesy of Joan Keefe.)

54

Fr. Robert Barrett was a showman, architect, and artist. He designed the underground shrine to be modeled after the catacombs of Rome. Its entrance was a rocky, vine-covered hill with a life-size bronze crucifix. The church was adorned with decorative rock formations and objects of art on its walls. Light shone through skylights onto hanging plants and vines. There were shrines to Our Lady of Lourdes, St. Anthony, and other divine figures. From the ceiling were suspended cages that held singing canaries. A manger scene depicting the birth of Christ with 12 statue figures was on display year-round. The photograph shows the main altar within the underground church. (Courtesy of Joan Keefe.)

Father Barrett purchased the land adjoining the shrine and built three chapels there: Sacred Heart, Mother Cabrini, and the Miraculous Medal. This was followed by the construction of a rectory and surrounding gardens. The chapels were ornamented like the underground shrine, with light coming from crystal chandeliers. Barrett claimed that the floor of the Miraculous Medal contained a stone from each of the 32 counties of Ireland. It was not unusual to have 10,000 to 15,000 people visit St. Anthony's each weekend. On Monday mornings Barrett would walk to Oceanside National Bank with his St. Bernard dog, which carried the Sunday collections in a bag around its neck. The picture shows the church grounds, with Lincoln Avenue toward the left and Atlantic Avenue toward the top. (Courtesy of Joan Keefe.)

Michael Orzano came from Italy at the turn of the century. He and his wife, Josephine (Milone), had a farm on the corner of Lincoln and Perkins Avenues. Orzano raised cows and made cheese, which, by horse and buggy, he brought to Brooklyn to be sold. After World War I, he and his family went into the construction business. The Orzano family has long been deeply involved in community affairs and in the development and character of Oceanside. Seen here are, from left to right, Pauline, Michael (with Pat on his lap), Joe, Theresa, Josephine, Anthony, and Mary. (Courtesy of Dr. Michael Orzano.)

The fourth fire company organized was Southside Hose Company No. 2, in July 1927. Its 32 charter members originally met at Salamander Fire Hall. Their temporary headquarters was Linus Anderson's garage on Mott Street. Linus rang the fire bell by hand. The board of fire commissioners gave Southside a Ford hose and a well-equipped chemical truck. The company's permanent headquarters was built on Oceanside Road, south of Mott Street. This picture was taken c. 1930. The men seen at the right are Charles Bedell (front) and Monford Bacon. (Courtesy of Nikki Wright.)

On May 6, 1928, on a seven-acre site purchased from Florence M. DaCosta, part of which was Foster's Dairy Farm, the cornerstone of South Nassau Communities Hospital was laid. The hospital opened its doors on November 12, 1928, and within a month had admitted 81 patients and delivered 18 babies. One of the proponents of the hospital was nurse Mary Pearson, seen here, who was instrumental in a $250,000 fund-raising drive for the 50-bed hospital. She was the hospital's first superintendent and a nurse there for 51 years. George A. Combes was the hospital's first administrator. (Courtesy of Maria Heller.)

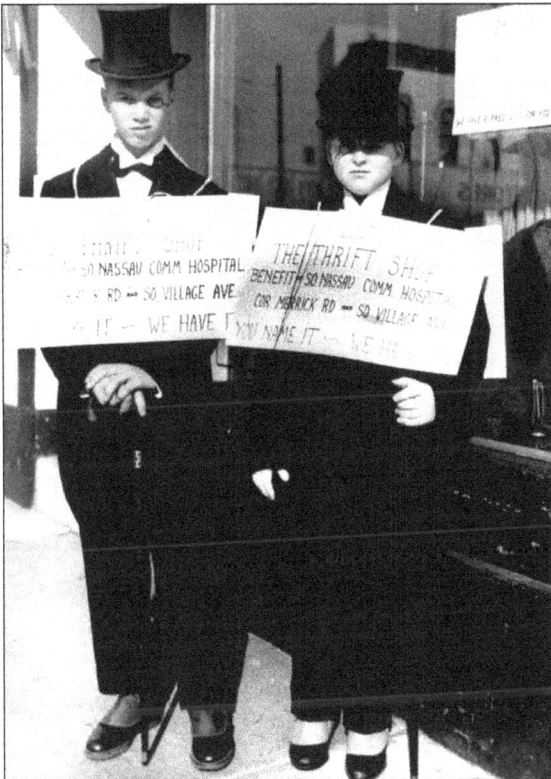

Women's auxiliary groups were continually trying to raise money for the hospital by running bazaars, bridge parties, and cake sales. The president of Oceanside's auxiliary was Clara K. Intemann. Other Oceanside citizens involved in fund-raising and development were Mr. and Mrs. Christian Binner, Sanford A. Davison, Rufus H. Smith, Sanford Story, Taylor Johnson, Paul Ayres, Edwin R. Burtis, and Ernest Vandeweghe Sr., who was elected South Nassau Communities Hospital president in 1962. The boys shown here are advertising for the hospital's thrift shop. The hospital currently employs 2,200 people and delivers 1,500 babies each year. (Courtesy of Thom Larsen.)

Morris Chwatsky arrived penniless in New York City from Poland in 1913. When he moved to Oceanside, he delivered newspapers, and sold socks and pants to his clients. In 1921 he married his Polish girlfriend, Bluma, and in 1924 she and his two sons came to the United States. In 1927 the Chwatskys (with brother Herman "Hymie") opened Oceanside General Merchandise Store on the southeast corner of Davison Avenue and Long Beach Road. Most of the business was done door-to-door. The picture shows Hymie ready for business behind the wheel of the store's truck. The name of the store was later changed to Oceanside General Variety Shoppe. (Courtesy of Joe Chwatsky.)

As business grew, the store spread north, until the Chwatskys owned a building. Chwatsky's was *the* store in Oceanside—the place to buy everything: from a single needle to a household of furnishings; from a diaper to a burial suit. It was where you bought your gym clothes, or an outfit for your first communion or bar mitzvah. The Chwatskys were the first well-known Jewish family to live in Oceanside. They and their employees treated customers as neighbors. The store continued in business until 1996. (Courtesy of Joe Chwatsky.)

At the end of 1927 voters rejected a proposal to erect a new high school, but bond issues for additions to School No. 2 and for the construction of a new elementary school were approved. The new building was constructed on Oceanside Road, across from South Nassau Communities Hospital. Construction for School No. 5 (pictured) began in the fall of 1928 and was completed the following year. (Collection of the author.)

Willow Dairy was run by the Hendrickson family, and occupied different areas in Oceanside where the Hendricksons' cows grazed. One area became the church property of St. Anthony's. Another was in front of Terrell Avenue School No. 2. The cows would graze the grass in front of the school, all the way across to the area where Brian Street is today. Seen here are George Hendrickson and a bull in front of School No. 2. Terrell Avenue was named for Oscar Terrell, an ancestor of the Hendricksons. (Courtesy of Pete and Dorothy Hendrickson.)

In the 1920s airplanes became the rage. Between Long Beach Road and Lawrence Avenue there was an airstrip where Oceansider Bert Shields offered 10-minute sightseeing rides for $2 in his airplane, *New Moon*. Shields was president of the Sunrise Flying Club of Oceanside. When an airport was opened in northeast Rockville Centre, he landed the first airplane on it to prove that the ground was suitable. The airport was christened by breaking a bottle of water against Shields's plane. (Collection of the author.)

Oceanside Harbor, Oceanside, L. I.

Oceanside, bounded on the south, west, and east by bodies of water, has always been a place for boating enthusiasts. From those bodies of water extend creeks, canals, and channels. Many Oceanside residents love to spend a day fishing, sailing, water-skiing, or jet-skiing. This photograph comes from a 1928 postcard showing Ocean Harbor in southwestern Oceanside. The body of water is the East Rockaway Channel. (Courtesy of Tracy Noon.)

Oceanside's fifth fire company, Terrace Hose and Chemical Company No. 3, was founded on June 13, 1928, by a small group of men who met at Hennenlotter's Grocery Store, 52 Nassau Parkway. The company's first truck was a Model T hose wagon, and its initial job was to respond to calls to add additional hose line. Then, in 1931, the company got its first pumper, an American LaFrance. Shown here is an Ahrens-Fox pumper. Terrace is part of the first-response unit for calls in northern and eastern Oceanside. Its motto is "First Due from the North." The company's headquarters is on Columbus Avenue. (Courtesy of Kevin Kline and Mark Babich.)

Capt. Lou Pearsall (left) was Oceanside's resident marine expert. He started working for the U.S. Coast Guard when he was 15 years old. He was there to assist in the rescue of the *Princess Anne* from the Rockaway shoals. Pearsall was an expert in boating, marine life, tides, fishing, shipwrecks, and carpentry. He lectured frequently, and wrote many articles for the *Long Island Forum*. His legacy endures in his writings, taped speeches, and collections. Here, Pearsall is preparing to go out for a day of duck hunting with Bill Swan (middle) and Ira Pearsall (right). (Courtesy of Arthur and Audrey Pearsall.)

John Colquhoun is seen here as a young boy, holding his cat while standing in the backyard of his house on Nassau Parkway in the 1920s. He grew up to become an insurance agent in Oceanside. Colquhoun and his wife, Sara Stead, had three children. Sara Stead, whose father, Ebor Stead, worked as a trolley driver, was Oceanside's resident seamstress and taught sewing classes at the high school. Behind Colquhoun in this picture can be seen two significant characteristics of Oceanside at the time: the vast expanse of land and the family outhouse. (Courtesy of Sara Colquhoun.)

As the decline of the oyster industry coincided with the advent of Prohibition, some baymen became rumrunners. It is said that "Anyone in Oceanside who owned a boat was in the business." The community had speakeasies and stores selling the ingredients for making alcohol. The *New York Times* wrote that more than 300 rumrunners worked the shores from Oceanside to Seaford. It also reported that Oceanside and its neighbors had a "rum inflow greater than any section in the country." Rumrunning was dangerous. On March 23, 1929, a body washed ashore in Oceanside near a shack with a still. Reporters called the death the result of "a bootleggers' feud." (Courtesy of Greg Schreier.)

Speakeasies, where liquor and gambling abounded, were equipped with avenues for quick escape. Oceanside's speakeasies had names like the Rat Hole and the Snake Pit, both located on Long Beach Road. At Oceanside Beach there was the Casino, and on Atlantic Avenue, bordering the water, was Duffy's Tavern (above). Duffy's was owned by "Big Bill" Duffy, a manager of world heavyweight champion Primo Carnera. In private homes, people were also caught by the "booze patrol." The Lemily house on the corner of Roosevelt Avenue was raided. The Lemilys' horse stable had a trapdoor that led downstairs to a still. Their kegs were axed, and alcohol flowed into the street. At Hotel Miramar in Oceanside, some less-than-honest policemen and politicians are said to have kept the alcohol flowing before the place was raided toward the close of the 1920s. Proprietor Lora Murray pleaded guilty, and was sentenced to six months in jail and a $500 fine. (Courtesy of Pam DeBaun.)

On Roosevelt Street near Lincoln Avenue was the farm of Arthur Banks Noon, the son of Adam and Hannah Noon, who had a farm on Christian Hook Road. Arthur Noon married Laura Denton, and they had 12 children. The eight boys of the family worked the farm, while the mother and the four girls cleaned, cooked, and canned vegetables and fruit. According to the youngest son, Tracy Noon, morning chores included milking cows, feeding and watering horses, and chopping wood before school. Afternoon chores were cleaning and bedding the stables, sifting coal, and plowing the fields with horses. (Courtesy of Tracy Noon.)

Arthur Noon, shown here, cut hay all the way to Long Beach Road and around his property. He also cut hay at the Meadows in southern Oceanside. Noon did not own all that land, but people were happy to have their land cleared. Rufus Smith used to have Noon cut the hay in a field near his house so that his grandchildren could play football. Hay was used not only for fodder, but also for traction on the roads and for keeping ice solid in icehouses. Noon also grew vegetables and raised chickens, pigs, and goats. (Courtesy of Tracy Noon.)

64

TUTING'S CHICKEN FARM, Oceanside, L. I.

Chicken farms existed in town longer than did traditional farms. Residents age 50 or older all remember at least one near their house. The ad for Suessman's farm appeared in the *South Shore Observer* on January 19, 1919; "Stop 96" refers to the trolley stop on Brower Avenue. The postcard was from Tuting's Chicken Farm. (Courtesy of the Oceanside Library.)

Shown here is the back of the Burtis house on Ellen Terry Drive, with the family horse, Willie. On this homestead were grown the tastiest peaches around. Edwin and Helen Burtis lived on the farm with their 11 children. They had a carriage house, a barn, and a milk-cooling house. They were among the first households to have a telephone, and neighbors would come over to make a call. Son Joe Burtis was the sole graduate of Oceanside High School in 1919. (Courtesy of Mr. and Mrs. Emil Kuster.)

In the 1920s Harry H. Baumann's farm was at 27 Brower Avenue, near Stop 98 on the trolley line. Harry Baumann was a printer, but his farm was famous for its fresh eggs, corn, strawberries, and rhubarb. A fruit and vegetable booth stood in front of his house and the other Brower Avenue farmhouses of the Soper, Gulick, Peace, and Burtis families. The Baumann family was passionately concerned with community improvement and intimately involved in community affairs. The photograph shows the trolley going down Brower Avenue. The house in the foreground is gone; the house in the background is the Baumanns'. (Courtesy of the Baldwin Historical Society.)

Six

THE DEPRESSION
AND THE 1930S

From June 1928 through the mid-1930s, retired Wall Street financier Charles W. Beall owned a zoo—one of the world's largest private zoos—on 10 acres south of Mott Street. Here, the millionaire thrilled youngsters by giving rides on elephants, giant turtles, and llamas. The zoo also had snakes, rare birds, lions, tigers, leopards, bears, and jaguars. There was a dance pavilion on the grounds, and on summer nights the sounds of the festivities mingled with animal calls. Elephants were paraded tail-to-trunk to cool off in the famous "elephant hole" (shown here), while daring boys and girls swam nearby. From time to time monkeys would escape and climb onto the roofs of nearby houses. When the zoo closed in the late 1930s, most of the animals wound up at Frank Buck's Zoo in Massapequa. Charles Beall died in his house on the zoo grounds in February 1939, at age 67. The land was inherited by the stage actress Ninon Bunyea, who rented the buildings to Frank Buck and an animal importing company, Weens Brothers and Ward. (Collection of the author.)

67

Harry Baumann was considered Oceanside's unofficial mayor. He wrote and edited speeches for local politicians and was the force behind the formation of the Oceanside Sanitation Commission. His wife, Emma, was involved in starting the school hot lunch program and in the formation of Oceanside's first library. Harry was chairman of the local Welfare Committee. This picture shows those involved in a performance that was part of a government work program. Pictured are, from left to right, Baumann, Ruth Dibble, Phil Higley, Walter Ward, and William Postance (director). (Courtesy of the Queens Borough Public Library, Long Island Division.)

The Oceanside High School girls basketball team, under the coaching of Ruth Lewis, won seven championships in 10 seasons, from 1929 to 1938. Her field hockey team lost only one game from 1933 to 1935. Starting in 1925, Miss Lewis taught physical education to every girl in Oceanside's school district. She started the tradition of Girls' Sports Night. See here are, from left to right, the following: (first row) Beverly "Dot" MacDonald, Virginia Shea, Catherine Anson, Sarah Stead, Ellen Gallagher, and Alice Dovel; (second row) Coach Lewis, Florence Smith, Clara Roettger, Dorothy Hemmer, Margaret Smith, Evelyn Brodie, Jessie McAuslin, and Florence Gaiser. (Courtesy of Sean Keenan.)

During the Depression era of the 1930s a national craze arose for "walkathons," which were actually dance marathons. It was a time when people needed cheap social entertainment, perhaps with a chance at winning a small prize. Couples would enter a walkathon and dance for days. The last couple dancing (standing) was the winner. Oceanside walkathons were held in a club called Dean's, across from the Roadside Rest, or in the building on the northwest corner of Long Beach Road and Mahland Place. That building is still in existence; at various times it was the site of a Good Humor distribution plant and of a roller skating rink. The couple shown here are obviously posing for a picture before the start of the marathon. During the Depression many Oceanside families were in need of food. Canned goods and other packaged foods were collected by the American Legion "Feed a Family" drive. Kathryn "Kitty" Strang, a local activist and politician, worked for the Oceanside Welfare Committee, which operated out of the post office, then located on the corner of Long Beach Road and Anchor Avenue. (Courtesy of the Queens Borough Public Library, Long Island Division.)

In the spring of 1931 the finishing touches were put on the Oceanside Golf and Country Club. The 175-acre course included the area where Oceanside High School and Middle Bay Golf Course are today. Sponsors of the course felt that a golf club was needed for middle-class people who couldn't afford Long Island country club dues. The course was the site of both amateur and professional contests. One prominent golfer was George Ramsden; another resident pro was Jack Oliver, who owned a driving range where East Bay Diner now stands. The clubhouse shown here stood on the corner of Waukena and Skillman Avenues. (Courtesy of Stuart Williams.)

MONSTER BENEFIT

FOOTBALL CONTEST
Under the Auspices of

PARAGON CLUB

Entire Proceeds for the

JOINT WELFARE COMMITTEES
of Baldwin and Oceanside

PARAGON CLUB

vs.

BAYVILLE A. A.

SUNDAY AFTERNOON, NOVEMBER 29, 1931
BALDWIN HIGH SCHOOL FIELD
Church Street and Grand Boulevard

Music by
AMERICAN LEGION DRUM CORPS
BALDWIN POST NO. 246

Tickets, 50c Per Person

From 1929 through 1936 Oceanside had a semiprofessional football team called the Paragons. They played at Soper Field, south of Foxhurst Road, and also at Bristol Field, located where Nathan's is today. They attracted crowds of up to 6,000 people. The team consisted of players from Oceanside and local towns. Oceansiders on the team in 1931 were Earl "Tim" Bristol (captain), Kemp "Tex" Kaye, Howard "Howie" Baumann, Robert Wulbern, and John Vandermosten. At left is the cover of a program from one of the games. (Courtesy of Al Pasetti.)

Many Oceanside boys enjoyed the organized sports provided for them by the St. Anthony's Catholic Youth Organization. The program was initiated by Fr. Joseph O'Connell and continued by Fr. Herbert McElroy, who came to St. Anthony's in 1938. McElroy coached the teams and would load them into his car and drive them anywhere they needed to go for a tournament. There were football, baseball, and basketball teams, all nicknamed the Anthonians. Howie Baumann (pictured), son of Harry H. Baumann, was a star football player at Oceanside High School and a successful coach of the Anthonians. (Courtesy of Frank Januszewski.)

You did not have to be Catholic to be an Anthonian. Oceansider Arthur Wright remembers a time when the starters of the basketball team were two Methodists, two Presbyterians, and Phil Shapiro, who was Jewish. Seen here are the Anthonian "Juniors" of 1941. Note the "A" on the uniform of Thompson, the captain, who is holding the ball. The others are, from left to right, Edwardson, Williams, Olsen, Le Fevre, and Murray. Members of the second team, not pictured, were Ousterman, Welsford, Whitestone, Pearsall, and Blum. (Courtesy of Frank Januszewski.)

Before 1930, Lutherans in Oceanside worshiped at Holy Trinity Church on Lincoln Avenue in Rockville Centre or at Terrell's Hall. Oceanside's first full-time Lutheran Pastor was Rev. T. Rene Meyer, who was installed at Easter in 1931. The Lutheran Church building on Davison Avenue was dedicated on February 23, 1936. The first cash donation for the building fund came from Fr. Robert Barrett of St. Anthony's Parish. This is a picture of the church from Fairview Avenue. (Collection of the author.)

In the spring of 1933, Earl Towers purchased Gilda Gray's estate for $18,000. He then went into the mortuary business. An essential part of the success of Oceanside's Board of Trade, Towers was a founding father of Oceanside Rescue Company No. 1. The family business, carried on by Earl's son Robert Towers, has been serving Oceanside for 70 years. Shown here are Earl Towers (left) and Herbert Adorno, who ran a fuel company and was a member of Kiwanis and of the Board of Trade. (Courtesy of Gladys Jacobsen.)

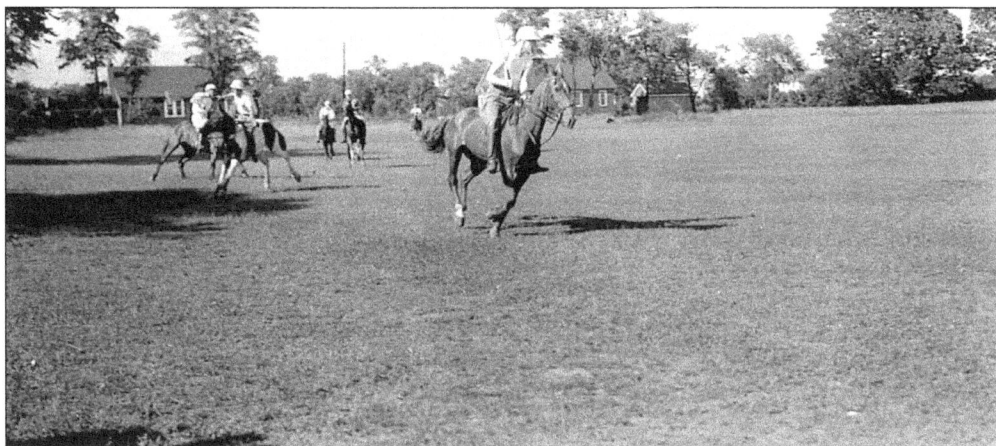

A sport that gained popularity during the 1930s was polo. In Oceanside, games were played behind Salamander Firehouse at Brower Field, also known as the Polo Field. Games on Sunday mornings were well attended. Some of the horses were kept at local farms. Older children would be allowed to walk the horses during rests from their shifts. This picture shows a match in progress at Brower Field. Oceansiders who played polo there included Jack McCumiskey, Charlie Helmcke, Alfred DeMott, and Chubby Moffett. Oceanside High School won the indoor polo championship in 1938. (Collection of the author.)

In 1930 the population of Oceanside was 5,838 and rising. In 1936 a new high school was built for $414,000, and the former high school became the junior high. At the dedication ceremony, held on October 14, 1936, Supt. S. Taylor Johnson (pictured) gave the dedicatory address and the high school orchestra played "Pomp and Circumstance." Students were happy with the new building but were not as happy about the time allotment for classes, which now lasted 45 minutes instead of 30 minutes. (Courtesy of the Oceanside School District Archives.)

73

Charles R. Mosback was an admired leader in the Oceanside School District—a teacher, a coach, and high school principal from 1940 to 1963. Oceanside High School's football field and Athletic Hall of Fame are dedicated to Mosback. Under his picture in the Hall of Fame is this inscription: "Charley Mosback was a coach who inspired his boys to play fair, preserve in defeat and be magnanimous in victory." Here, Mosback sits in front of his "boys." Behind him is Charles Helmcke, who became a principal in the Oceanside School District. (Courtesy of Mike Limmer.)

Davidson Ave. and Long Beach Road, Oceanside, Long Island, N. Y.

Oceanside's "102 village" had modernized, as seen in this postcard. Progress was evident in the paved sidewalks and the gaslights on poles in the triangle. The area bustles with cars. From this vantage point we can see a stationery store, a shoe store, a barbershop, Bohack's, and Whelan's Drugs. On the next corner is the bank. The modern streets no longer show the trolley tracks. (Courtesy of Brian Merlis.)

The Triangle Business Centre of Oceanside, Long Island, N. Y.

This is the "102 village" looking north. The boys, dressed in knickers, pose outside the cigar store. A shoe store can be seen on the west side of the street; across the street are a taxi service, candy store, dairy, and Roul's, which may have been a restaurant. A penny scale stands outside the stationery store, which sold Hoffman Beverages, Optimo cigars, and Reid's ice cream. (Courtesy of Brian Merlis.)

At a PTA meeting on March 8, 1937, citizens suggested starting a community library. Mrs. Oliver Wright became chair of the library committee. Funds were raised through tag sales, donations, and card parties. Rufus Smith offered a small building, and Abe Levin offered a spot next to his drugstore. The Oceanside Jewish Sisterhood donated a flag, and the high school's vocational class made the library's sign and bookends. Librarian Marion Sanger did the book classifications. The library opened on February 22, 1938, with Thomas Fetherston, president of the school board, cutting the ribbon. Pictured here in 1941 is our second library on Davison Avenue. (Courtesy of Tracy Noon.)

The place to stop for candy or supplies on the way to school was Mitchell's Luncheonette, also known as the Canteen. It was located on the southeast corner of Foxhurst and Oceanside Roads. Lunches at Mitchell's cost a quarter. The luncheonette had a jukebox, and teenagers danced there after school. (Courtesy of Tracy Noon.)

Over the railroad tracks, south of Atlantic Avenue on Bayview Avenue, was the Knickerbocker Ice Company. This 1935 picture shows a part of the building that still exists. Before electric refrigeration units were available, families used iceboxes to keep their food from spoiling. In the background is Paul's Boat Works, offering boat storage and repair as well as other marine services. (Courtesy of the Queens Borough Public Library, Long Island Division.)

PUCKER BRUSH HILLBILLY BAND
FROM BUNDY CENTRE
Petes Stable, Long Beach Rd., Oceanside, L. I.

Pete's Stable offered refreshment, music, and dancing. Owned by Pete Ungerland, it was on the east side of Long Beach Road, just north of where the movie theater now stands. Shown here is the Pucker Brush Hillbilly Band. (Courtesy of Joe Trapani.)

Down the road from Pete's Stable was Mammy's Chicken Farm, offering Southern fried chicken, to eat inside or to go. At night, Mammy's offered drinks and dancing. The picture of Mammy (left) is representative of the times. (Courtesy of Joe Trapani.)

Abe Levin, who generously donated the land next to his store for the library, was the resident druggist. His store in the village not only filled prescriptions but also, like many drugstores in those years, had a luncheonette counter and served ice-cream sodas. Levin's took over Whelan's Drugs and, as seen here, for a time the store sign bore both their names. The first drugstore in Oceanside was Chubbuck's. (Courtesy of the Oceanside Annual.)

On a muddy Oceanside field, on November 19, 1938, in front of 7,000 rain-soaked fans, the high school football team played Valley Stream Central for the Nassau County championship. Bleachers were set up in a "bowl" fashion around the field, and 100 uniformed Oceanside firemen were on hand for crowd control. In the third period, Bela Rieger drove in from the five-yard line for the only score, and Oceanside finished the season unbeaten and untied. First Team All-Scholastics were Bob Adrian (center) and Steve Poleshuk (guard). Steve, who later became Oceanside High School principal, was the only Long Island player selected for the All-Metropolitan Team. He became an All-American at Colgate. Second-team All-Stars were Dick McLean (tackle), Bela Rieger (fullback), and Ray MacDonald (halfback). The team, voted best on Long Island, won the Rutgers Cup. Seen here are, from left to right, the following: (standing) Jack Coons, Dick McClean, Charles Hudson, Bill McCumiskey, Bela Rieger, Bob Pearsall, Steve Poleschuk, Ray MacDonald, Gordon Niddrie, and Bob Hopkins; (kneeling) Bob Adrian with mascot, "Billy." (Courtesy of Frank Januszewski.)

This happy group is at a football pep rally in the 1940s. Straddling the side of the car is Harold Haff, who later became town superintendent of highways. The driver is Jack McCumiskey, football player and future owner of Jack's Pony Ring. The "Bill" on the side of the car is for Billy Bowers. Pictured are, from left to right, the following: (first row) Gloria Gottleib, Harold Haff, Selma Klossman (teacher), and Jack McCumiskey; (second row) two unidentified persons, Billy Bowers, and Gilbert Davies. (Courtesy of Frank Januszewski.)

Oceanside's Only Newspaper

The Oceanside

HOME NEWS

Printed and Published In Oceanside

East Rockaway   Island Park   Baldwin   Oceanside   Rockville Centre

Vol. III, No. 29 — Six Pages.   THURSDAY, MAY 22, 1941   Price Three Cents

ANNUAL PARADE ON MAY 30

High School Band Will Give Concert At Jones Beach

Want Women To Register for National Defense

Legion, Many Others to March In Honor of the War Dead

OCEANSIDE, N. Y., May 22.—It is expected that the Memorial Day parade in Oceanside will be bigger and better than ever this

In the late 1930s and early 1940s Oceanside had its own newspaper, the *Oceanside Home News*. The publisher was Daniel Caroline. The paper contained local news, personals, and advertisements. Through the personals you learned who was getting married, who had been born, and who had died. You also learned who was entertaining guests and where people were vacationing. An item in the September 5, 1940, edition reads, "Mr. and Mrs. Jack Fenley of Hoke Avenue are entertaining Mr. and Mrs. J. V. Hollis and their daughter Mary Jane for the week." (Courtesy of Jeanne Simmons.)

The New York World's Fair of 1939–1940 was held in Flushing Meadows, Queens. The biggest and most expensive World's Fair of its time, it took as its theme "Building Tomorrow with the Tools of Today." Those who spent 75¢ to attend on April 30, 1939, had the treat of seeing television for the first time, as Pres. Franklin Roosevelt gave the first televised presidential address. Those who spent 75¢ to attend on May 18, 1939, had the treat of watching the Oceanside High School Band play in front of the Washington Statue at 3:00 p.m. The photograph shows members of the band congregating around that statue. (Courtesy of Jeanne Simmons.)

Leading the Oceanside Band at the World's Fair was James R. Day, who worked for the Oceanside School District from 1934 to 1967. Day started the first marching band at Oceanside High School. He also wrote the school's alma mater, which originally was sung to the tune of "Clementine." Later, John Race wrote new music. (Courtesy of Jeanne Simmons.)

Dr. Walter Boardman served for 12 years as Oceanside's high school principal and 20 years as its superintendent. He was a Scout leader and an avid outdoorsman who excelled in target shooting and, in 1957 walked the Appalachian Trail. After his retirement, Boardman became an environmental activist. He lobbied for the conservation of wetlands and to establish the National Trail Act. He was appointed executive director of the Nature Conservancy in March 1961. In 1972 he moved to Florida, where, because of his work to save marshland from developers, the Volusia County Council named a street after him. When the town decided to cut trees down to create a new bridge across Walter Boardman Lane, he was the first to protest. One of those trees held a plaque to his partner in environmentalism and in life—his wife, Elizabeth Boardman. (Courtesy of the Oceanside School District Archives.)

Advertised as "Long Island's Family Rendezvous," the Roadside Rest on Long Beach Road became a Long Island institution. The little fruit stand opened by Morton Shor and Murray Hadfield in 1921 evolved to a frankfurter and soda stand and then into a beautiful Spanish-style building with a booming food and entertainment business. During the day, it was a stop-off point for those traveling to and from the beach at Long Beach. (Courtesy of Erich Haesche.)

The Roadside Rest, with a seating capacity of 4,000, featured legendary bands of the 1930s and 1940s, such as Tommy Dorsey, Benny Goodman, and Lionel Hampton. People danced under the stars in the open-air pavilion. To listen and dance to Benny Goodman cost 50¢; on Saturdays the price jumped to 75¢. (Courtesy of the Queens Borough Public Library, Long Island Division.)

At the end of the 1930s, a subtle change occurred at Oceanside High School. Up to that time there had been no official nickname for high school teams, though newspapers would refer to an Oceanside team as the Siders. But as the 1940s began, people started referring to the team as the Sailors. Credit for the new name is given to Joe DeBaun, a student and cheerleader who graduated in 1938. He began wearing a sailor suit to the games, where he led cheers through his megaphone. DeBaun met his future wife, Edyth, during a football game, while she was cheering for the Woodmere team. The DeBauns were active business and community leaders in Oceanside. (Courtesy of Frank Januszewski.)

Oceanside Beach, Oceanside, Long Island, N. Y.

Older residents giggle when they talk about swimming in Middle Bay, better known as "B. A. Beach." The more modest would swim at Oceanside Beach, which was located on the other side of town, on the southwestern border of Oceanside, along the East Rockaway Channel. Near the beach were small bungalows, bathhouses, and stores, as well as a large building known as the Casino, where people could get a hot dog or a soda and adults could go at night for entertainment. (Courtesy of Joe Trapani.)

A short trip down the road from the beach was the Silverleaf Hotel, where visitors could make a vacation out of their stay. Oceanside Beach had its own lifeguard crew, led at one time by Bill Baumann. In the water was a large raft with diving boards. The house in the background sold pickles and candy. Shown here at the beach, c. 1940, are, from left to right, Barbara Foster Comfort, Clarence "Happy" Prutting, and Jean Turner Ravalli. The girl on Happy's shoulders is unidentified. (Courtesy of Jean Ravalli.)

Some of the biggest names in Oceanside's history celebrated Townsend Southard's 80th birthday on September 1, 1939. Seen here are, from left to right, the following: (first row) Blanche Jobe, Andrew Southard Sr., Mabel Ellen Southard, Townsend Lee Southard, Andy Southard Jr., unidentified, Marion Snyder, unidentified, and Mary Vandeweghe; (second row) five unidentified persons, Mr. Foster, John T. Snyder, and Howard Haff; (third row, starting with the young man poking his head up) Ernest Vandeweghe Sr., two unidentified persons, Rufus Smith, Percy Southard, Clarence Southard, Sanford Story, George Hill, and Harry Snyder. John Snyder owned the New Bootery. Mr. Foster owned Foster's Dairy Farm, the site where the hospital was built. George Hill owned the gas station at the corner of Davison and Oceanside Roads. Ernest Vandeweghe was a prominent resident. His wife, Mary Smith Vandeweghe, was the daughter of Rufus Smith. (Courtesy of Andy Southard Jr.)

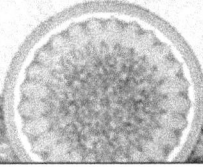

Frederick W. Shaw was a leading citizen in Oceanside. Born in 1887, he was educated in Oceanside and received his undergraduate and law degrees from Syracuse University. He returned to Oceanside, where he became the school district's attorney and the second president of Oceanside National Bank. Shaw's wife, Eleanor Pearsall, was the daughter of the famous Oceanside oyster dealer Alexander A. Pearsall. Seen here is an original Oceanside Bank stock certificate purchased by Shaw. (Courtesy of Joe Trapani.)

This photograph shows the Triangle. In the background is Smiles, a five-and-ten-cent store. Next to it stands the A&P. An electric pole and light are visible, as are some automobiles. Vanella's Funeral Home now occupies the area where Smiles and the A&P once stood. (Collection of the author.)

Seven

THE WORLD WAR II YEARS

Gene Charles Isaac (pictured), an Oceanside High School graduate who excelled in sports, was a member of the 302 Infantry Regiment, 94th Division of the American Third Army. Isaac was killed in action in Germany on February 19, 1945. Another local hero of World War II, Sgt. John A. Kissell, was killed in North Africa; he received a posthumous Silver Star that was accepted by his father at a ceremony on Governor's Island, New York, on October 14, 1943. Kissell, former salutatorian of Oceanside High School, was cited for reorganizing all of his men into rifle squads when their mortar ammunition was expended. The Oceanside post of the Veterans of Foreign Wars is named after Kissell. Another Oceanside casualty was war correspondent Kenneth Brown Collings of 40 Stevens Street. Collings was an aviator; his book *Just for the Hell of It* (Dodd, Mead & Co., 1938) told of his exploits in flying. Although he was over 40 years old, Collings volunteered to ferry troops overseas. (Courtesy of the Oceanside High School Library.)

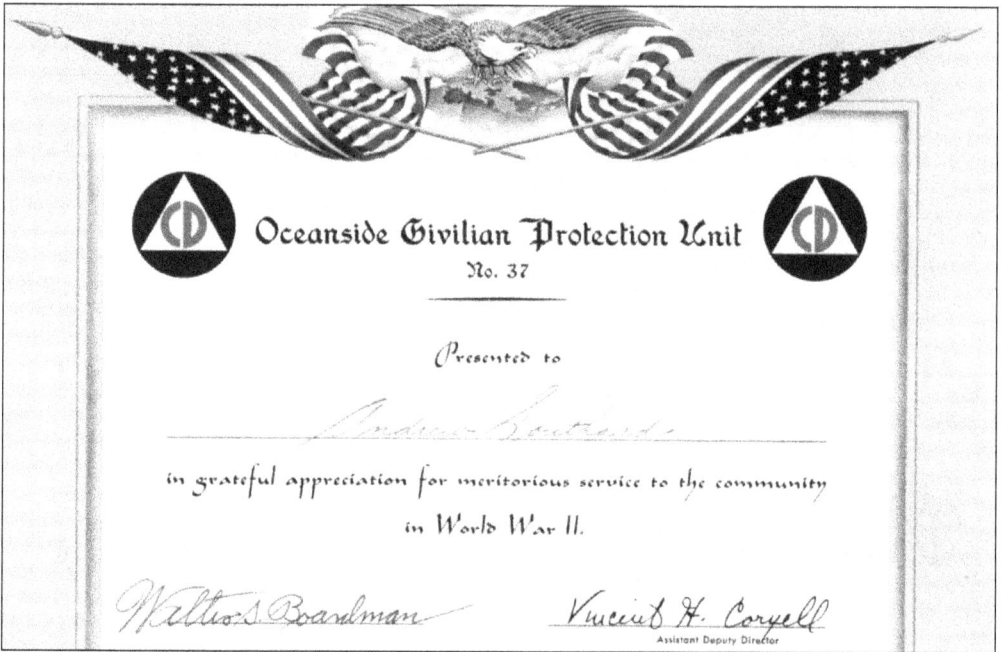

Oceanside Civilian Protection Unit

No. 37

Presented to

Andrew Southard

in grateful appreciation for meritorious service to the community

in World War II.

Walter S. Boardman

Vincent H. Coryell
Assistant Deputy Director

Many men and women in Oceanside sacrificed themselves in military service. Hundreds from Oceanside served, including Sgt. Arthur L. Pearsall, who was in the air transport command in India. Al Shea served in the 10th Mountain Division in Italy. At least 54 servicemen from Oceanside gave their lives, including Bob Rachofsky, who died on his first day in combat. Another war hero, Capt. George E. Bourguignon of 51 Weidner Avenue survived the flying of 118 missions, including the Battle of the Bulge. Alexander H. "Hughie" Jack was a sergeant and paratrooper. In April 1944 he was reported missing in action and later was declared a prisoner of war. In May 1945 he was liberated. Jack was famous for greeting people by raising his fist and saying, "Yea, Oceanside!" Other citizens at home served as civil defense agents, running air-raid drills and devising plans for protecting citizens in case of attack. The certificate in the picture was given to Andrew Southard Sr. for his work in the Oceanside Civil Protection Unit. (Courtesy of Andy Southard Jr.)

Oceansiders' lives changed when the country entered World War II. Meat, gasoline, and other necessities were rationed as people were urged to sacrifice for the common good. Schoolchildren went through air-raid drills and wrote letters to soldiers overseas. William T. Morris of 125 Foxhurst Road, who made spokes for ship steering wheels, was honored with a Labor Merit Badge. Oceanside had its own "Rosie the Riveter" in Beverly Ridgway, who worked as a riveter at Grumman Aircraft Corporation. Her husband, Sgt. Robert Ridgway, was killed in action. The photograph shows Ed Hynes, ex-POW, leading the Memorial Day parade. After the war, Oceanside had a parade down Long Beach Road that was led by movie star Virginia Mayo. (Courtesy of Ed Hynes.)

One of Oceanside's largest businesses was Bristol Motors, which sold Ford automobiles. Run by the Bristol family, it was on Long Beach Road, where Marty's Shoes now stands. All of the driver education cars used by the high school came from Bristol. After World War II the Community Father's Club, with members John Vandermosten and Fred Thomforde, among others, reactivated Oceanside Youth Activities Inc. It sponsored biweekly dances on the second floor of the Bristol Motors building. The floor also became a recreation and drop-in center. The teenagers set it up with a jukebox and decorations and dubbed the youth center "Sailor's Haven." (Courtesy of the Oceanside Annual.)

Ernest "Pal" Vandeweghe was an athletic star at Oceanside High School. He graduated in 1945 and was granted football scholarships to the University of Michigan and to Annapolis, but he decided to play basketball at Colgate instead, after that college mailed him a key to the dorm. Ernie Vandeweghe became an All-American. During college vacations he practiced with the New York Knicks, and after college he attended Columbia Medical School and played for the Knicks. Many nights Ernie would arrive just as the game began because he was attending a class. He played for the Knicks for seven years and then practiced medicine in California. (Courtesy of Frank Januszewski.)

In 1947 Theodore Messler (pictured) opened a hardware store on Long Beach Road. Messler Oceanside Hardware was one of Oceanside's legendary stores, a mom-and-pop operation with solutions to all household problems. For 50 years the Messlers served the community. Organized and immaculate, their store seemed unchanging; to enter it was to take a walk back in time. Although there was an old-fashioned cash register, Mrs. Messler would always pull the pencil out from behind her ear and do the math for a checkout on a brown paper bag. (Courtesy of the Messler family.)

One tradition that lives on in Oceanside is the Memorial Day parade. Veteran soldiers, firefighters, civic organizations, and bands march through the streets, to the delight of old and young. In some years close to 4,000 have marched. The photograph shows Oceanside twirlers in one of these parades, c. 1946. Seen here marching down Davison Avenue toward Woods Avenue are, from left to right, Ellen Mischo, Gloria Sweeney, Miriam Higgins, and Sally Baldwin. (Courtesy of Ellen Lucas.)

BOB BAUMANN'S KIDDIE KLUB AND SUMMER DAY CAMP   Playgrounds and Classrooms
27 Brower Avenue, Oceanside, Long Island, N. Y.

In 1947 Bob Baumann opened a nursery school at the Baumann Homestead. Originally called Bob's Kiddie Klub, it eventually became Camp Baumann, a summer day camp for children 6 to 13 years old. Many school personnel, including Arthur Wright, Steven Poleshuk, and Bob Sodemann, worked for Baumann. At the summer camp, kids enjoyed sports, horseback riding, arts and crafts, swimming, woodworking, dancing, drama, and miniature golf. Some residents remember Bob riding his horse around the swimming pool. (Courtesy of Bob Baumann.)

Bob Baumann started buying and using his own buses as transportation for his camp. When Walter Boardman asked him to bid for the school transportation contract, he won, and his bus company began. The Baldwin, Rockville Centre, and Freeport school districts were next, and others followed. The company grew into one of the largest businesses in Oceanside. Although Baumann sold the bus company in 1982, if you ride through the South Shore of Long Island today, you can still see buses with the Baumann name on them. (Courtesy of Gladys Jacobsen.)

Oceanside Rescue Company No. 1 was established in 1947. Its mission is to provide citizens with emergency medical service. One of its first ventures was to start a blood bank at South Nassau Communities Hospital. Rescue Company members donated blood and urged others to do the same. Members of the Rescue Company, who are certified in CPR and first aid, respond to over 1,000 calls per year. Currently the Rescue Company's headquarters is on Tilrose Avenue. One of their first trucks (with floodlight) is pictured. (Courtesy of Bill Lynch and Pete O'Neill, Oceanside Fire Department.)

Eight

THE 1950S AND THE 1960S

Oceanside Little League was organized in 1950 by Bob Baumann and local Brooklyn Dodger scout Mickey McConnell. Baumann's father, Howard, acquired a Little League charter and became the organization's first president. The Little League started with four teams of boys, ages 10 to 12; games were played on the camp property on Brower Avenue. Another organizer was Arthur Wright, a former Oceanside student-athlete and an Oceanside physical education teacher. Many days Wright would have to coach both teams and umpire the game as well. He said, "It always went well until I got into an argument with myself." Oceanside produced its share of local and regional champions, as well as three Major League pitchers. All-Star Dennis Leonard of Kansas City, John Costello, and John Frascatore all made it to the "bigs." Leonard won 146 major league games. Costello was 11 and 6 with a 2.97 ERA for his career, and Frascatore won 20 games over seven years as a middle-reliever. (Courtesy of Sean Keenan.)

In the 1930s a Jewish citizens' group hired a teacher to prepare children for bar mitzvah, but Oceanside had no temple. About 40 families set out to rectify this, and in 1948 Oceanside Jewish Center was officially incorporated, with Herman Schwartz as its first president. In 1949 the first Jewish service was celebrated at the Evergreen Firehouse. That same year, the OJC purchased the Soper family's farm on Brower Avenue. The temple was dedicated on March 18, 1951. Samuel Gluck was the original contractor for the building; the first full-time rabbi was Elihu Kasten. Here the temple is seen as it appears today. OJC now has a Hebrew school, a banquet hall, auxiliary clubs, and a preschool. (Collection of the author.)

The Catholic fraternal organization Knights of Columbus began in Oceanside in 1952 with 50 charter members. It was named after Fr. Joseph O'Connell, a parish priest who worked with young people. The first Grand Knight was Andrew Hickey. From 1952 to 1961 meetings were held at Evergreen Firehouse. In 1961 ground was broken at Kenneth Place for a new hall, lounge, and administrative building, which opened on November 4, 1962. According to Frank Ford, a charter member, the Oceanside Council has 2,300 members, making it the largest in New York State, and supports 35 different charities. The photograph shows the Long Island Softball Champs of 1959. Seen here are, from left to right, the following: (first row) Ed Molloy, two unidentified persons, Tony Argila, Vincent Gerardi, Tom Waters, Angelo DeLibero, and Tom DiDominica; (second row) Pat Carr, Dick Woods, Fred Gunther, Jack Spiller, unidentified, Ed Boyle, Frank Ford, unidentified, Mickey Pizzani, Bob McAdams, and Chuck Zanni. (Courtesy of Frank Ford.)

One of the country's best outboard motorboat racers was August Nigl, a sheet metal worker who also repaired and built boat engines. Nigl lived next to the canal on Park Avenue. In 1950 he won the 18th annual Hudson River Marathon from Albany to New York City, and also set a new speed record. His sleek yellow 50-horsepower boat was named *Forever Amber*. The prizes Nigl took home included a silver plaque, a television, an atmosphere clock, a movie projector, a movie camera, and a new Plymouth automobile. The photograph shows Nigl, after the Hudson River Marathon, sitting on his new car and holding his championship trophy. (The cute girl in the hat is his daughter Diana.) Nigl also won the first boat race around Long Island. (Courtesy of Sheila Nigl.)

The Oceanside Stallions have provided boys with football, wrestling, and roller hockey teams. Seen here is the logo of Oceanside Little League Football. (Courtesy of Pete O'Neill.)

LITTLE FOOTBALL

OCEANSIDE STALLIONS A.C.

Age 8 - 14

OFFICERS

PETE O'NEILL .... PRESIDENT

JOHN BARRY .... FIRST VICE PRESIDENT

In 1951 a boy named Tommy DiDominica started selling lilacs on Sundays in front of his parents' house on the corner of Lincoln and Atlantic Avenues. His father, Thomas DiDominica Sr., saw him prosper and bought his son trays of daffodils. Tommy sold these and also began selling potted plants. While he was still in high school, his table of flowers grew into many tables under a tent on his parents' property. After high school DiDominica attended Farmingdale College, where he studied horticulture. He bought a piece of property adjoining that of his parents and began to grow his own shrubs. Eventually a building and a greenhouse were erected. DiDominica and his wife, Adele, made the business thrive. The picture shows the construction of the greenhouse. Dee's Nursery is now famous for selling quality merchandise, giving expert advice, and holding one of the largest sales in the country every Fourth of July. (Courtesy of Tom DiDominica III.)

After World War II Oceanside had another population surge as new residents poured in from New York City and elsewhere. In 1950 the population was about 18,000. Homes were built in many of the vacant lots; land that had been worthless could now be developed at a profit. In southern Oceanside hundreds of acres of marshland were filled with millions of cubic yards of fill. The growth rate was great. From 1951 to 1957 about 3,400 houses were built. The photograph shows suburban kids playing"Ring Around the Rosy" on Ocean Harbor Drive. The homes there were built at the end of the 1950s. (Courtesy of Susann Ross.)

Those who wanted to bowl could go to Oceanside Bowl, located where New York Sports Club is today. It held leagues, and the high school's bowling team practiced there. There was a luncheonette counter where you could get a sandwich and a Coke. Oceanside's other bowling center was C&J Bowl, located on the corner of Long Beach Road and Weidner Avenue. C&J, a popular place with teenagers, burned down on January 7, 1971. Bowlers smelled "rubber burning," and then the ceiling of alley number 16 collapsed. The fire raged for ten and a half hours. (Collection of the author.)

In 1949 Edyth and Joe DeBaun opened a nursery school on Atlantic Avenue. It soon became a day camp known as Camp Wonderland. Campers enjoyed field trips and rides on a wagon pulled by the horse, Wonderboy. Kids could boat in man-made Willow Lake, ride go-karts, swim in the pool, ski on a straw hill, or even get a haircut. "Uncle Joe" could be seen during the day wearing a funny hat, walking on stilts, or riding his unicycle. For more than five decades Camp DeBaun has been inviting kids to be part of their family and to enjoy the pleasures of being a child. Here, Edyth is seen at back left and Joe at back right. (Courtesy of the DeBaun family.)

In 1949 Roger Folz started a company with one pistachio nut machine. He expanded the business to small independent vending machine routes. Then, a few years later, Folz changed his focus to national chain accounts and made his business a national leader in the bulk vending industry. Today, Folz Vending employs 262 people and operates 140,000 vending machines. At age 76, Roger still works daily in his office. His philanthropy is noteworthy: Folz generously supports many charities, sponsors local youth teams, and gives annual athletic sportsmanship, social studies, and business scholarships to seniors at Oceanside High School. (Courtesy of Roger Folz.)

In the 1950s many Jewish families bought homes in the new housing developments in southern Oceanside. In 1952 a group of these Jewish families formed a new congregation and purchased a beautiful old homestead on Oceanside Road. They used the house as a Sunday School and converted a carriage house into a place of worship. Dr. Charles Ozer was the first rabbi of Temple Avodah, which grew into one of the largest Reform temples in Nassau County—and which may have been the first temple in Jewish history to appoint a woman cantor, Mrs. Sheldon Robbins. The photograph shows Temple Avodah as it appeared in 1955. (Courtesy of the *Oceanside Annual*.)

The Oceanside Recreation Department was started in 1954 and was propelled to prominence by its first director, Joseph E. Curtis. It has provided the community with many services, including education, sports, community events, and summer camp. This photograph shows coach, teacher, and recreation leader Charlie Murphy during a boxing lesson. To the left is Henry Brinkman; to the right, John Asher. The Recreation Department, now the Department of Community Activities, offers classes in art, technology, and CPR, and provides numerous programs for children. (Courtesy of the Oceanside Annual.)

One Recreation Department tradition is Halloween "window painting." Kids paint store windows on Long Beach Road; they decorate the windows with witches, jack-o'-lanterns, ghosts, or fall harvest scenes. At one time, kids painted all of the storefront windows from the northern border of Oceanside to Atlantic Avenue. Although the paintings are now done on mural paper, as seen here, originally they were painted directly on the windows. After painting, there sometimes was a ragamuffin parade from Poole Street to the junior high school grounds. Prizes were awarded for costumes and paintings. (Courtesy of the Department of Community Activities.)

Before malls there were shopping centers. In 1954 Oceanside got the Great Lincoln Shopping Center. Its principal tenants became F. W. Woolworth, Food Fair, and National Shoes. Before the shopping center was erected, the site was used for a yearly carnival and for tournaments by firefighters. The photograph shows an advertisement for the grand opening of Food Fair on July 13, 1955. (Courtesy of Lia's Pizza.)

The Oceanside Fire Department has won many tournaments over the years. This picture shows the men around their "C rig." Seen here are, counterclockwise from the front, Al Schmidt, George Arrandale, Ed Widdick, Charlie Mahler, Fred Robinson, Walter Arrandale, Harvey Husser, Joe Short, Alan Chandler, Bill Gildea, Ken Hyder, and Bucky Combs. (Courtesy of Pete O'Neill.)

With the postwar baby boom in full explosion, it became clear that a new high school would be needed. When the Oceanside Golf and Country Club closed in 1947, 35 acres west of Skillman Avenue were purchased. The new high school boasted ample laboratory space for science, special rooms for theater and industrial arts, a modern cafeteria, and a gymnasium that could hold 1,000 people. Seen in this photograph of the cornerstone ceremony from October 3, 1954, are, from left to right, Andrew Southard, Walter Boardmann, Thomas Fetherston, Charles Goldie, Earl Borgerson, and Neil Sager. The school was dedicated on September 1, 1955. (Courtesy of Andy Southard Jr.)

Oceanside Recreation ran its first "Oceanside Day!" on June 7, 1958. It consisted of sporting events, bait-casting demonstrations, art, displays of hobbies, a pie-eating contest, and dancing. The event would be re-created in a similar format in 1984 as "Oceanside Alive!" Conceived by Paul Press and brought to fruition by Doris Chwatsky, Morton Horowitz, and many other community members, Oceanside Alive!—a day of music, dance, arts and crafts, and games for children—became an annual event. In this photograph, a crowd of participants wearing Oceanside Alive! T-shirts are seen in the parking lot of Nathan's. (Courtesy of the Department of Community Activities.)

The OCEANSIDE BEACON
The Only Newspaper In The World Solely Interested In This, Your Community.

In 1954 the first *Oceanside Beacon* was published. The *Beacon* offered community news and Oceanside events, with sections for personal, recreation, and political news, as well as advertisements. It provided a place for local residents to voice their opinions on school and local politics, and for civic organizations to post advertisements for their events. For years the *Beacon* was Oceanside's official newspaper. Today the local newspaper is the *Oceanside/Island Park Herald*. (Courtesy of Jeanne Simmons.)

The photograph shows Alfred Pasetti as a young boy with his family in front of his father's candy store in Freeport. Pasetti and his wife, Serafina, opened an ice-cream and confectionary store on September 15, 1953, on Long Beach Road, diagonally across from Oceanside Bank. The store was quickly recognized for its delicious homemade ice cream. The Pasettis gradually increased the amount of food served until their store became a luncheonette. It became a place for teenagers to go after school to play the jukebox. In fact, so many teens crowded into the store that Pasetti got rid of the jukebox, upsetting one teenager so much that she ordered another. When the jukebox was delivered, Pasetti was not amused. (Courtesy of Al Pasetti.)

Pasetti's evolved into a cozy, popular family restaurant, where teachers from the school district went every day for lunch. This started a tradition so strong that if Pasetti's ever had to close, school would close, too. Frederick Shaw, Oceanside National Bank president, ate lunch at Pasetti's every day. No matter what the special was, he'd say, "Bring it on!" The Pasettis sponsored Little League Baseball and United Soccer. The restaurant closed on September 26, 2003. Rumor has it that, on that day, daily customer Art Wright took his lunch-counter stool home with him. (Courtesy of Al Pasetti.)

Johnny Russell is seen at the near end of his bar in Johnny Russell's Little Club on Long Beach Road. Other prominent businesses include Ocean Side Industrial Cleaners, Janowski's Hamburgers, Mel's Lincoln Stationery Store, and Sal's Shoe Repair. Vince Conti, the son of the family that runs Sal's, played Sergeant Rizzo in the television show *Kojak*. (Courtesy of John Russell.)

From its first politicians to Jeff Toback, the district legislator, Oceanside has had a hand in politics. In the 1800s Joseph Brower ran for town supervisor. Joseph Mount of Oceanside was one of Theodore Roosevelt's Rough Riders. Nora Cuddihy, a Democratic organizer in the 1920s, was admitted to the Nassau County Democratic Hall of Fame in 1975. In the 1950s and 1960s residents said that if you wanted to "get things done," you should talk to Harold Haff, the superintendent of highways, and F. Wright Donnelly, the sanitation commissioner. In the photograph, signs for Haff and district court judge John Daly are held by members of Oceanside's Women's Republican Club. (Courtesy of Eileen McCabe.)

106

Carvel soft ice-cream stands were popping up everywhere in the 1950s. This picture shows the opening night of Carvel on Long Beach Road in 1954. The Niccolicchia family owned this Carvel stand and kept it open into the 1990s. (Courtesy of Barbara Schnitzer.)

In 1955 some families proposed an Orthodox Jewish temple in Oceanside. Services were held at 23 Davison Avenue, above a laundry store. In 1956 land was purchased on the corner of Waukena Avenue and Oceanside Road. Rabbi Benjamin Blech was chosen as the spiritual leader. At the groundbreaking ceremony held in 1959, New York State assemblyman Joseph Carlino was the guest speaker. The first service in the new temple was held on May 14, 1960. The synagogue started with a Talmud Torah Hebrew School, youth clubs, and cultural and social activities.

In 1956, Murray Handwerker acquired the Roadside Rest property. He learned the restaurant business working for his father, Nathan Handwerker, of Nathan's Famous of Coney Island. On June 4, 1959, after some refurbishing, the restaurant reopened as Nathan's Roadside Rest. (The name was eventually modified to Nathan's Famous.) In addition to "the world's best hotdogs," Nathan's had hamburgers, seafood, sweet corn, soft ice cream, and thick French fries. Nathan's was every youngster's pick for a birthday party. A handful of dimes equaled hours of fun in the Game Room, shooting targets and playing pinball. (Courtesy of Nathan's Famous.)

Nathan's was the place to stop on the way to or from the beach—barefoot, sandy, with or without a shirt. Grandparents took the little ones there for ice cream after a day next door at Kiddieland Park. On Monday there was square dancing, on Tuesday jazz (later, motorcycle night), on Wednesday Dixieland music, on Thursday opera, and on weekends kiddy shows. "Nathan's" was the first word mentioned after someone spoke of Oceanside. In 1976 Murray Handwerker sold the property. As many of those who were looking on shed a tear, a demolition crew finished knocking down the original building on June 11, 1976. (Courtesy of Jeanne Simmons.)

Arthur Heyman led Oceanside High School to a county championship in soccer and basketball in the 1958–1959 season. Later, at Duke University, he averaged 25 points and 11 rebounds per game over three years. In his senior year he was College Player of the Year and MVP of the NCAA Tournament. In the NBA draft he was selected No. 1 overall by New York. His first season, he was named to the All-Rookie Team. Heyman played for the Knicks, the Cincinnati Royals, and the Philadelphia 76ers. In 1967 he jumped to the American Basketball Association, where he and Connie Hawkins led the Pittsburgh Pipers to the championship. In 1990 Duke retired Heyman's number. (Courtesy of Sean Keenan.)

During the 1958–1959 school year, Oceanside won the county championship in soccer, basketball, track, and baseball. The baseball team was led by pitcher Howie Kitt, 17-0 that year, who later got a $100,000 bonus to sign with the New York Yankees, the highest signing bonus to that time. Kitt was given a parade and the keys to his hometown. Here he is shown with Yankees manager Ralph Houk in 1961. (Courtesy of Sean Keenan.)

On March 25, 1960, a fire caused by a short circuit in the electrical organ blazed for four hours, destroying the famous St. Anthony's Underground Shrine and its priceless religious artifacts. More than 300 firefighters from Oceanside and neighboring towns fought the blaze and were able to rescue a tabernacle and a crucifix. As firefighters, including Pete O'Neill (seen here handling the hose), flooded the underground church with water, statues floated out onto the street. To accommodate the parish's families for Mass, temples, firehouses, churches, and Oceanside Bowl offered their buildings. (Courtesy of the Oceanside Fire Department.)

In April 1960, in a house on Oceanside Road, a lithograph of the Virgin Mary holding the Christ Child was the focus of amazement and curiosity. Mary was producing tears. Hundreds lined up to gain a glimpse of the "miracle," and a procession carried the icon to St. Paul's Greek Orthodox Church in Hempstead. The picture "wept" for over five weeks. (Collection of the author.)

110

In 1960 residents petitioned for a park to be built in Oceanside. The Oceanside Recreation Coordinating Council, led by Al Shapiro, selected 20 acres in southern Oceanside, and in September 1961 the town of Hempstead acquired the land. Oceanside Town Park has a playground, four baseball fields, and three basketball, six handball, and four tennis courts. In 1965 a pool complex was added adjacent to the park. (Collection of the author.)

The Oceanside Fire Department Band, a perennial winner of band contests, marches in September 1960. Among its members were Michael and Anthony Orzano, Bill Van Wickler, Bill Moyer, Red Robinson, Russ David, and Kenny and Lenny Gibfried. (Courtesy of Dr. Michael Orzano.)

Feeling the impact of its final growth spurt, Oceanside expanded School No. 2 and added an elementary and junior high school. School No. 2 was renamed Florence A. Smith School in honor of its longtime principal. In September 1962, 960 students entered the new elementary and junior high school, which was named after Walter S. Boardman. Pictured from left to right are Ford Stone, superintendent; Florence Smith; John Vandermosten, school board president; and Carol Sewell, Smith's successor. (Courtesy of Tom Capone.)

OCEANSIDE USA !

On consecutive Saturday nights in April 1960, members of the community performed a musical titled *Oceanside USA!* in front of capacity crowds at the high school auditorium. The show—the brainchild of concerned citizens who wanted to bring attention to the town's library—featured songs and dances centering on the theme of "books." *Oceanside USA!* was produced by Arthur Iger, William Hauser, and Judith Wax and was written and directed by Desley Schwartz and Jewel Brodsky. The music was composed by Marvin Paymer, and the choreography was by Grace Wakefield. Every civic, religious, social, business, and fraternal organization was involved. (Courtesy of the *Oceanside Beacon*.)

On September 21, 1961, some 1,200 people attended the dedication of the St. Anthony's School building. Cornerstones were laid at the school and the new convent. Pastor Dennis E. Finn voiced his hope that "Catholic education will be an influence for good in this area." In the first year there were two classes each in grades 1 through 4. In the second year nuns from Blauvelt came, and two fifth-grade classes were added. The presence of the school, after the demise of the underground shrine, gave the parish a lift. New organizations arose, and so did bingo. The photograph is of the first graduating class to complete grades one through eight. The school closed after 1972. (Courtesy of Joan Woods.)

At the end of 1961 the town of Hempstead voted to build Oceanside's Refuse Disposal Plant in an area with houses, a school, and a park. Presiding supervisor Palmer D. Farrington said that this "carefully run operation . . . would not cause a burden to homeowners." The plant was the first in the country to use its waste heat to generate electricity. The adjoining landfill attracted seagulls and emitted odors. Through efforts by many civic activists, including David Sandler, Thomas Scopelitti, and Mark Raphan, the Town and the state Department of Environmental Conservation reached an agreement, and Oceanside's 160-foot landfill-mountain closed in May 1988. (Collection of the author.)

Oceanside United Soccer Club was founded by Joe Goldberg in 1962, with one team of 15 boys. Phil and Bessie Lamonica, whose late son, Rudy, was an outstanding soccer player, instituted girls' soccer in 1973. Since then, the club has grown to include hundreds of men, boys, and girls playing year-round. Oceanside's first professional soccer player was Ron Attanasio, who played for the New York Cosmos. Adrian Gaitan played in the World Cup. (Courtesy of Jaclyn Brandi.)

The biggest bear on Long Island in the 1960s was 15 feet tall, stood on its hind legs, and could be seen on an Oceanside front lawn. It belonged to Dr. Arthur "A. J." Marsh, a local dentist residing at 3159 Oceanside Road, who carved the bear out of a blight-stricken elm tree. The bear, a favorite of residents and woodpeckers alike, could be seen in the winter wearing a scarf and earmuffs. (Collection of the author.)

114

The Oceanside Post Office was on Anchor Avenue in 1928. In 1938 it moved to Poole Street and in 1952 to the corner of Smith Street and Long Beach Road. In 1962 the new post office on the corner of Atlantic and Lincoln Avenues opened for service. The building was dedicated on January 6, 1963, with 500 residents in attendance. Harold Haff officiated and Ernest Abrams, Oceanside's first mail carrier, raised the flag as the high school band played "The Star-Spangled Banner." (Collection of the author.)

The Jewish Center of Ocean Harbor, a Conservative synagogue, opened on March 2, 1963. Led by Rabbi Robert Schechtman, the congregation used the Knights of Columbus hall on High Holy Days. A temple with a sanctuary, meeting hall, offices, and classrooms was built in 1968 on the northeast corner of Weidner and Royal Avenues. Pictured is the Ross family—from left to right, Ronald, Susann, Lisa, and Wendy—in front of the temple. (Courtesy of Susann Ross.)

In 1963 Oceanside joined the effort to bring about equality among the races by starting the Oceanside Committee on Human Rights. Its president, Raphael "Ray" Klein (pictured), was head of the Human Rights Committee at the United Nations. The Oceanside organization conducted workshops, presented speakers, and spoke to high school students about violence and bullying. On August 28, 1963, members participated in the March on Washington to promote the passage of civil rights legislation. In 1965, when five college students from Oceanside were arrested in Alabama while taking part in voting-rights demonstrations, the Oceanside committee helped raise money for their bail. Other Oceanside activists included two young men who were part of the Freedom Riders organization. In Jackson, Mississippi, Joseph McDonald and Kenneth Schilman were arrested at the bus station for sitting in the Negro waiting room. (Courtesy of Ray and Roslyn Klein.)

During the Vietnam War, peace vigils and counterdemonstrations were held at the Triangle. From Oceanside, Maj. Vincent R. Harter received the Air Force Medal for aerial achievement. Naval Lt. Jefferey Harris received the Armed Forces Honor Medal 1st Class. Pictured here is Bob Patton from Oceanside's class of 1962. His Vietnam unit was army Company A, 43rd Signal Battalion, 1st Signal Brigade. (Courtesy of Bob Patton.)

William H. Wallace (pictured) received the Silver Star for gallantry in action in 1966. After his company leaders were killed, Wallace relayed commands given to him via radio from an injured battalion commander. After 22 hours, his battalion was rescued. Another hero, Marine Lt Daniel McMahon, commander of D Company, 4th Marine Regiment, kept his cool under enemy fire after an ambush. He and his troops spent three days in the jungle hungry and thirsty until rescue troops arrived. Corp. Peter Penfold, a marine, was among those from Oceanside who gave their lives. He was killed in action October 7, 1967. (Courtesy of the Oceanside School District Archives.)

In Oceanside's class of 1969, Bobby Iger was voted Most Enthusiastic. He was the president of Key Club, was sports editor for the newspaper, acted in a school play, and was an announcer at sporting events. Iger became a television executive at ABC, working his way up to become president of ABC Entertainment. In 1993 he became senior vice president of Capital Cities/ABC, and eventually was named their president and COO. Today he is the president of Disney. (Courtesy of Arthur and Mimi Iger.)

Another 1969 Oceanside graduate was future major league All-Star pitcher Dennis Leonard, who played baseball in high school for Andy Scerbo and at Iona College for Gene Roberti. He won 146 games for the Kansas City Royals, including three 20-win seasons. He pitched in the All-Star Game and in the World Series. Leonard is in the Royals' Hall of Fame and the Missouri Athletic Hall of Fame, and was an inaugural member of Oceanside's Circle of Pride. (Courtesy of the Oceanside School District Archives.)

From 1927 to 1968 Island Park's high school students attended Oceanside High School. In September 1968 this process began to be phased out, supposedly as a result of overcrowding. The real story involved the so-called Battle of Hog Island, a dispute over tax revenues from Long Island Lighting Company's power plant on Hog Island, on the border of the two communities. In 1965 the Island Park School District's boundary changed so that the power plant fell within Island Park's borders. Island Park did not pay tuition for its students during the 1968–1969 school year because anticipated tax revenues from the power company were held in escrow. After that Oceanside stopped accepting Island Park students; the last ones were in the class of 1969. (Collection of the author.)

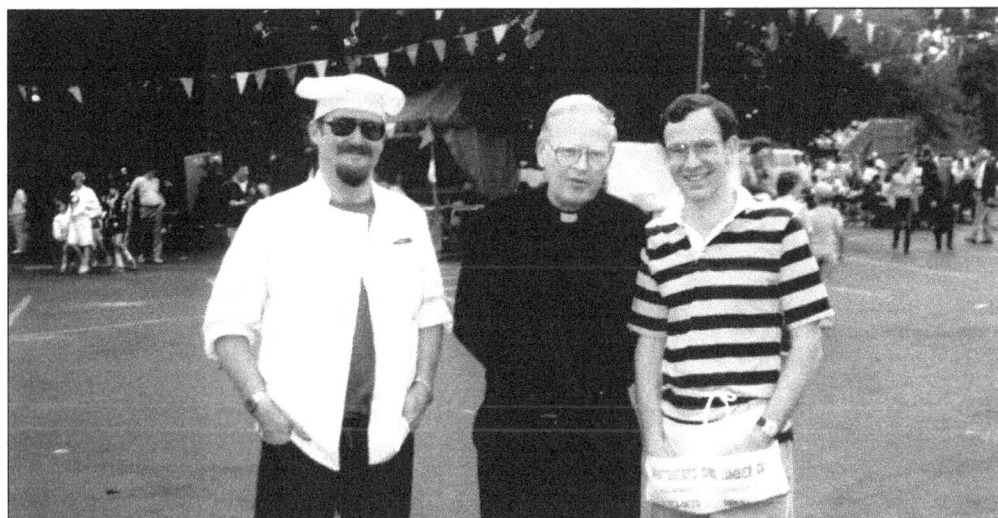

On June 13, 1970, the first St. Anthony's Feast was held—a night of dancing and celebrating, with games and delicious Italian food. Today, the feast is among the community's best events. It starts on Friday night and continues until Sunday afternoon. Pictured here are St. Anthony's priests at the feast in 1985; from left to right, they are Fr. Pierce Brennan, Fr. Joe Austin, and Fr. Vinnie Sullivan. (Courtesy of the Flannery family.)

Oceanside High School students had strong feelings about the Vietnam War. In 1970 the senior class voted by a two-to-one margin to have Congressman Allard Lowenstein, an outspoken critic of the war, as commencement speaker. A town controversy ensued. The board of education resolved that no candidate for political office would be allowed to speak. Some students boycotted graduation, and 200 of them held their own ceremony, with Lowenstein as keynote speaker, at the Laurel Theatre in Long Beach on June 20. Valedictorian Charles Adler proclaimed, "We must live by the values we mean to spread." Lowenstein used the words, "We are the majority of Americans not to be silenced." (Courtesy of Debbie Benjamin.)

The Oceanside chapter of Kiwanis Club International has existed since 1945. This service organization finances local teams, Boy and Girl Scout troops, school awards, college scholarships, and charitable causes. The photograph shows a tree-planting ceremony at Oceanside High School to honor past presidents. Seen here are, from left to right, Emil Janowski, Salvatore DiGiovanna, Alfred Shapiro, Fred Gropper, Joseph DeBaun, Stephen Poleshuk (principal), and Joseph Tanella. (Courtesy of Joe Murphy.)

Oceanside Community Service, organized in 1949, is still going strong, helping those in need of food, clothing, medical attention, and legal advice. The organization distributes layettes to expectant mothers and food baskets during holidays, as shown here. Its current leaders are Al Cullinane and Bob Transom. (Courtesy of Bob Transom.)

To celebrate the country's 200th anniversary, Oceanside held events that included a potluck luncheon, a Fire Department Band concert, an art show, a re-creation of British soldiers at war, and an authentic costume ball. Fire hydrants were painted red, white, and blue. Seen here is the Oceanside High School class of 1976, which buried a time capsule containing items from that time period. (It was dug up in 2001.) Speaking is class president Tami Hoffnung, with teacher James Mulvey behind her. (Courtesy of Jim Mulvey.)

Few love Oceanside as much as resident Tracy Noon, who considers himself the "oldest clam digger." He participated on the wrestling team at Oceanside High School and graduated in 1939. After school he worked for the town of Hempstead. Noon is always ready to lead a parade and will ride miles on his bicycle to see a sporting event. An avid collector of just about anything, he also loves to talk about hometown history. (Courtesy of Tracy Noon.)

Nine

BRAGGING RIGHTS

Oceanside High School won the New York State championship in baseball in 2000. Pitcher Bill Weitzman won all three games to secure the title, and he and teammate Nick Conte were selected as All-Americans. Catcher Brendan Harrigan was a pivotal player. Head coach Andrew Morris was selected as Coach of the Year for New York State. The picture above shows the team celebrating the Nassau County championship on their home field. The team consisted of Keith Van Wickler, Bill Weitzman, Brendan Springstubb, Pat Chambers, Dan Williams, Jared Florin, Frank Pisani, Ken Kobbe, John Jata, Jared Barry, Dom DiDominico, Jon Alto, Eric Mapplethorpe, Rob Schnabel, Jon Kourie, Joe Pumo, Dan Ingberg, Nick Conte, and Brendan Harrigan. The assistant coach was Richard Woods, and the junior varsity coach was Frank Nappi. (Courtesy of Andy Morris.)

On June 5, 1971, 17-year-old Susan Dishaw of Oceanside was named Miss New York State at Kutsher's Country Club in Monticello. The following October she competed in the Miss USA–World contest in Hampton, Virginia, wearing a Statue of Liberty costume and presenting the governor with a bottle of New York wine. She now teaches English and German at a Long Island high school. (Courtesy of Susan Weber.)

As an eighth-grader at Boardman Junior High School, David Paymer made his stage debut in the title role of Oliver. His father was a musician, his mother performed in community theater, and his brother was an actor. In high school Paymer was featured in the plays directed by drama coach Barry Kaplan, whom Paymer considers a major influence. After college Paymer acted on Broadway and appeared on television in shows like *Family Ties* and *Taxi*. He became a lead actor in major motion pictures, including *City Slickers*, *Payback*, *Nixon*, and *Mr. Saturday Night*. For his role of Stan Yankleman in *Mr. Saturday Night*, Paymer received a Best Supporting Actor Oscar nomination. (Collection of the author.)

Oceanside has had other great athletes and coaches in addition to those already mentioned. Seen here is Jay Fiedler, currently the quarterback of the Miami Dolphins. Don Castronovo holds the scholastic record for the 180-yard low hurdles. John Morley was a world champion wrestler. Robert Farb was a nationally ranked gymnastics champion. Fred O'Connor was a professional football coach with the San Francisco 49ers. Oceanside High School football coach Joe Scanella went on to win two Super Bowl rings as a coach with the Oakland Raiders. Oceanside people who have succeeded in the entertainment field, in addition to those mentioned previously, are Miramax Films vice president Barry Littman, actresses Mimi Saffian (*Go Ask Alice*, 1973) and Diane Farr (MTV's *Love Line*), television producer Glen Caron (creator of *Moonlighting*, with Cybill Shepherd), Broadway dancer Gregg Mitchell, renowned jazz pianist Ken Werner, and Phil Lang, a musician who was considered the "dean of American orchestration." Other noteworthy Oceanside natives are businessmen Charles Golub (former head of American Express), Randy Levine (president of the New York Yankees), Steven Friedman (former head of Goldman Sachs and now chief economic counsel to Pres. George W. Bush), and Warren Eckstein (world-renowned pet expert). (Courtesy of Frank Januszewski.)

The Oceanside High School Athletic Hall of Fame inducts alumni into the Circle of Pride, an elite group of athletes and coaches who have achieved greatness during and beyond high school. Sean Keenan and Tony Caiazza, who conceived of the idea, run an annual dinner ceremony at which the new members are inducted. The inductions are an extension of the work done by Frank Januszewski, who developed Oceanside's Athletic Hall of Fame with his own hands and his own money. Current members of the Hall are Dennis Leonard, Art Heyman, Ernie Vandeweghe, Patti Hanlon, Christine Andrews, Anna Meyer, Frank Januszewski, Angelo Plaia, John Morley, Jimmy Trenz, Melissa Pearsall, Jay Fiedler, Roy Chernock, Jill Januszewski, Ruth Lewis, Artie Wright, Andy Scerbo, Steve Poleshuk, Bill Pless, Charles Mosback, and members of the Lucas family (shown here), who have helped develop the community through housing, charity, and civic commitment for nearly 100 years. Lucas kin pictured here are, from left to right, as follows: (kneeling) Ken, Bob, and Jim Lucas; (standing) Jack, Steven, and Gary Lucas; and (inset) Ellen and Jack Lucas. (Courtesy of Frank Januszewski.)

Ten

THOSE WHO DIED FOR OTHERS

Seven members of Oceanside's Bravest have died while fighting a fire and attempting to save the lives and property of others. Dominick "Bubba" Lagudi (front and center) was one such hero. With him are, from left to right, Fred Wagner, Patrick Lagudi, and Bill Lynch, the current commissioner of the fire department. Others who have died in the line of duty are Thomas Staab, Joseph Jarvis, Vincent Herbert, Stephen Wade, William Koerner, and Anthony Zito. (Courtesy of Bill Lynch and Pete O'Neill, Oceanside Fire Department.)

Oceanside Servicemen Who Died for Others

World War I
Edwin Abrams
Francesco Molisse

Korea
Richard D'Errico

World War II
Harold Abrams
Charles Aubert
Bertram Audley
Guido Batteri
Harold Baylis
Ray Briney
Ray Brower
Joseph Buckley
Richard Burke
Milton Chwatsky
Harry Corbett
John Daly Jr.
George Dewey
Harry Dixon
Robert Downing
Hubbel Fellows
William Graham

Alexander Grant
Earl Griffen
Lewis Gritman
Edward Grohs
Robert Haig
Richard Hill
Edwin Hirsch
Wilbur Horsecraft
Gene Isaac
John Kissell
Frederick Kneipp
Bert Lang
Frank Lanzo
Carl Lindberg
Carman Magistro
Hugo Maiorana
George McNamee
Edmund Mitchell
William Mount
Leon Neoman
Frank Neu
Lendeth Noon
Jan Lier Oktavek
Lewis Oldmixon Jr.
Robert Rachofsky

Edwin Reilly
Robert Ridgeway
Russell Roach
Ralph Sankin
George Schaeffer
Harry Schneider
Nelson Sperling
George Story
William Trenz
Harold Tyers
George Vogel
Larry Wilson

Viet Nam
Harold Canan
Stephen Carlin
Dennis DeMichael
Russell Fauser Jr.
Ray Graham
Richard Heuffner
Adam Knecht
Ronald Maiorana
Raymond Meehan
Peter Penfold
John Rizzo Jr.

Several Oceanside citizens died during the attacks on the World Trade Center towers on September 11, 2001. Josh Birnbaum, seen here wearing his high school basketball uniform, was one. Others were Janice Ashley, James Barbella, John Florio, Thomas Gardener, Laura Giglio, Timothy Haviland, James Kelly, Kenneth Marino, Jeffrey Nussbaum, Robert Spear Jr., William Spitz, and Marc Zeplin. (Collection of the author.)